CONELY BRANCH
050174011

CERES
Celestial Legend
Volume 2: Yûhi

This volume contains the CERES: CELESTIAL LEGEND installments from Part 2, issue 1, through Part 2, issue 6, in their entirety.

STORY & ART BY YUU WATASE

Editor's Note: At the author's request, the spelling of Ms. Watase's first name has been changed from "Yû," as it appeared on previous VIZ publications to "Yuu."

English Adaptation/Gary Leach
Translation/Lillian Olsen
Touch-up Art & Lettering/Bill Schuch
Cover Design & Layout/Hidemi Sahara
Editor/William Flanagan
Shôjo Edition Editors/Elizabeth Kawasaki and Andy Nakatani

Editor in Chief, Books/Alvin Lu
Editor in Chief, Magazines/Marc Weidenbaum
VP of Publishing Licensing/Rika Inouye
VP of Sales/Gonzalo Ferreyra
Sr. VP of Marketing/Liza Coppola
Publisher/Hyoe Narita

© 1997 Yuu WATASE/Shogakukan Inc. First published by Shogakukan Inc. in Japan, as "Ayashi no Ceres."
New and adapted artwork and text © 2004 VIZ Media, LLC. All rights reserved.

No portion of this book may be reproduced or transmitted in any form or by any means without written permission from the copyright holders. The stories, characters, and incidents mentioned in this publication are entirely fictional.

The rights of the author(s) of the work(s) in this publication to be so identified have been asserted in accordance with the Copyright, Designs and Patents Act 1988. A CIP catalogue record for this book is available from the British Library.

Printed in the U.S.A.

Published by VIZ Media, LLC
P.O. Box 77010
San Francisco CA 94107

Shôjo Edition

10 9 8 7 6

First printing, January 2004
Sixth printing, October 2007

www.viz.com
store.viz.com

VIZ GRAPHIC NOVEL

Story and Art by

Yuu Watase

Aya is a boisterous, modern high school girl. On her 16th birthday, she's shown a mummified hand which causes powers to emerge — powers she doesn't understand. Her grandfather, the Mikage patriarch, declares Aya must be killed!

Tôya is a handsome but mysterious man who works for the Mikages, but he helps Aya escape from her family's murderous clutches on her birthday. He rescues Aya again when she tries to see her brother and the Mikage henchmen come after her.

Ceres is a legendary tennyo (celestial maiden) bent on revenge against the Mikage family for stealing her celestial robes (hagoromo), preventing her from returning to the heavens.

Aki is Aya's nice-guy twin brother who suffers multiple lacerations all over his body when he's shown the mummified hand. His grandfather orders him to be taken into protective seclusion as the heir to the Mikage empire.

Suzumi is a Japanese dance teacher with a connection to Aya. It's from Suzumi that Aya learns that she is a direct descendant of a celestial maiden with strong powers.

Kagami is the second-in-command of the Mikage corporation. His plan for Aya differs from Grandpa Mikage's.

Yûhi is Suzumi's martial artist/cook brother-in-law. Before he and Suzumi can rescue Aya from Aya's mother, who is wielding a kitchen knife and chasing her through their house, Aya transforms into the celestial maiden Ceres.

Grandpa is the patriarch of the Mikages and chairman of a vast corporation. He orders that Aya must be killed and Aki must be protected.

You may have noticed some unfamiliar people and things mentioned in Ceres. VIZ left these Japanese pop-culture references as they originally appeared in the manga series. Here's an explanation for those who may not be so J-Pop savvy:

Page 25: Mrs. Q. doesn't really look like the beautiful-but-frivolous Chisato Moritaka.

Page 43: A reference to the famous cook Rokusaburo Michiba from the infamously melodramatic cooking show IRON CHEF, which pits culinary geniuses against one another. His poster is hanging on the wall.

Page 44: The Ulfuls are an overly energetic, retro-sounding Japanese band.

Page 140: TOKIMEKI MEMORIAL is a dating RPG.

Page 145: TOKUMEI RESEARCH 200X ("Hot Topic Research 200X") is a sensational "scientific" news magazine show.

Page 145: TAKESHI NO BANBUTSU SOSEIKI ("Takeshi's Book of All Things Genesis") is an entertainment/pseudo-documentary show.

Page 145: ODORU DAISÔSASEN ("The Dancing Line of Criminal Investigation") and STALKERS: NIGEKIRENU AI ("Stalkers: Inescapable Love"!) are TV drama series.

Page 153: Mrs. Q's comment, "Porinky Porinky. Not gonna tell!," is a reference to a jingle from a popular snack commercial.

Page 153: Mrs. Q's name (Oda Kyu/Q-Chan) and appearance both pay comical homage to the classic anime series, OBAKE NO KYU-TARO ("Kyu-Taro the Ghost").

C...
CERES...?
YOU'RE... NOT AYA...?

THE EXISTENCE CALLED "AYA" WAS CREATED OVER THE COURSE OF THE LAST 16 YEARS.
HER CHARACTER IS MERELY A DEVELOPMENT OF HER SURROUNDING ENVIRONMENT AND INTERPERSONAL RELATIONSHIPS...
THE "CELESTIAL MAIDEN," THEN...
...IS THIS HER PERSONALITY TALKING NOW?
!
WE ARE NOT DIFFERENT. "AYA" IS ME... HAS ALWAYS BEEN ME.
IT'S JUST THAT THE FACET OF ME CALLED "AYA" WAS DOMINANT.
SHE IS THE FIRST OF THE MIKAGE DAUGHTERS IN A LONG WHILE WHOSE BODY IS ABLE TO BRING "ME" OUT THIS FAR...

ぎり...
A
O
K
YOU MUST BE ONE OF THE MIKAGES' MINIONS...
ガラ!!

TŌYA...
...!
.....
I MUST *DESTROY* THE MIKAGES, EVEN IF IT MAKES *YOU* MY *ENEMY.* WILL YOU *STILL* SIDE WITH THEM?
YEAH. I WAS TOLD TO BRING YOU BACK *ALIVE.*

I SEE...
THEN I SHALL BESTOW THE JOYS OF TRANSCENDENT BLISS...
...UPON YOU, AS UPON THE MIKAGE FAMILY.
!!

FLOWER PETALS...?
HEY! WAIT A SECOND!
THAT WOMAN IS ALSO A MIKAGE...
AND YOU WOULD PROTECT HER?
H...HOLD IT! STOP! THIS IS YOUR... I MEAN, AYA'S MOM!

DON'T BE AFRAID. YOU HAVE NOTHING TO DO WITH THE MIKAGES.
PLEASE STAND BACK. I DON'T WANT YOU HURT...
...YŪHI.
WHOOSH...

THAT'S NOT *AYA!* AYA'S RUDE AND OBNOXIOUS, NOT TO MENTION NOT A BIT GENTLE OR GOOD-LOOKING OR SEXY AT *ALL!*
YOU MEANIES!
THIS ISN'T A BIG HOUSE BY THE LOOK OF IT, BUT I CAN'T TELL WHERE I AM. HAVE I SLIPPED INTO...
...A DIFFERENT *DIMENSION,* MAYBE...?

?
A BALL...?
ぴゅ
ぽーん
ぽーん
ぽーん

CERES?
ARE YOU SURE SHE'S THE CELESTIAL MAIDEN?
DON'T THINK I'LL LET YOU GET AWAY.
WHERE ARE MY... "CELESTIAL ROBES?"
YEAH. IT WAS REALLY WEIRD HOW HER EYES AND HAIR COLOR CHANGED. SHE'S A TOTALLY DIFFERENT GIRL!
THUMP
YOU CAN DO IT! THE CREST ON THE BANDS YOU WEAR ARE INFUSED WITH MY POWER. SHE MUST RETURN TO NORMAL, BECAUSE IF SHE DOESN'T, WE'RE IN DEEP TROUBLE!
S... STOP HER? HOW?!
THEN YOU HAVE TO FIND HER AND STOP HER!

WHICH MIKAGE, BY BLOOD OR CONTRACT, KNOWS WHERE THEY ARE?
I CANNOT RETURN HOME WITHOUT MY ROBES.
I COULDN'T SAY.
I DON'T EVEN KNOW ANYTHING ABOUT *MYSELF.*
I SEE. IN THAT CASE...

WHAT ARE YOU DOING?! LET ME GO!
STOP IT!
YOU'RE AYA, NOT THIS "CELESTIAL MAIDEN!"
IF YOU INTERFERE, I WILL MAKE NO EXCEPTION OF YOU!
YOU WILL BE WIPED OUT ALONG WITH ALL "MIKAGE!"
THE MAN WHO TOOK MY ROBES AND VIOLATED ME IS OF THAT BLOODLINE...!
...!

!!
LIPS
A...
KISS...

TŌYA...
HM...?
.....
slap

A...
AYA?!
HOLY GEEZ, IT WORKED!
WHAT DO YOU THINK YOU'RE DOING, YOU PERV?!
WHAT ARE YOU TALKING ABOUT?!
WHAT THE HELL'S GOING ON WITH YOU?
OH!
TŌYA?!
WH-
WHY...?! GASP
WEEOOO WEEOOO

WEEOOO WEEOOO
HEY! OVER HERE!
WAIT...
!!
MOM...!
OH GOD, MOM WAS CHASING ME...TALKING CRAZY...
SHE COLLAPSED, AND WON'T WAKE UP...
MOM...
MOM... PLEASE, OPEN YOUR EYES!
WEEOOO WEEOOO
MOM!
WEEOOO

EXCUSE ME. HELLOOOO?

THANKS.
OH! SURE! I'LL ONLY BE A MINUTE...

YOU WANT SOME-THING, AKI?
I'M A BIT HUNGRY. COULD YOU BRING ME SOMETHING TO EAT?
I CAN'T GET OUT OF BED YET, SO...

"THOSE WOUNDS THAT APPEARED ON YOU... ARE PROBABLY AN EMBODIMENT OF HOW OUR ANCESTOR DIED..."
IF THEY THINK THAT EXPLANATION WILL MAKE ME STAY PUT...
HMPH! THEY STILL BELIEVE I'M AN INVALID, WATCHING ME 24-7 LIKE THAT.
WHAT KIND OF WIMP DO THEY TAKE ME FOR?
WHAT HAPPENED TO AYA?
WE KNOW THAT SHE'S WITH THE AOGIRIS...
YES, AND WE'LL SOON HAVE HER, GRANDFATHER.
GET HER... BEFORE AKI FINDS OUT!
WE'D BETTER! WE CAN'T RELAX WHILE SHE'S ALIVE!

UNIVERSITY HOSPITAL

IN A *COMA...?*

THEY SAY THERE'S NOTHING TO DO BUT LET TIME TAKE ITS COURSE.
.....

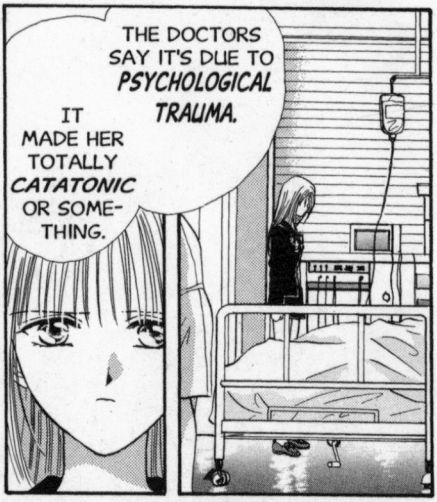
THE DOCTORS SAY IT'S DUE TO *PSYCHOLOGICAL TRAUMA.*
IT MADE HER TOTALLY *CATATONIC* OR SOME-THING.

"NO MATTER HOW MUCH GIRLS *RESIST*, ONE *KISS* AND THEY'RE *ALL YOURS!*"
HE'D THOUGHT OF THE LAST THING HE HEARD HIS FRIENDS SAY.
...OH NO...
BLUSH
ANYWAY, THIS CELESTIAL MAIDEN CALLED HERSELF CERES... NICE JOB GETTING AYA BACK, BY THE WAY.
QUICK THINKING.
I HAVE TO WONDER IF THE *MIKAGES* ARE BEHIND THIS. HOW CAN A MOTHER *ATTACK* HER OWN DAUGHTER...?
AND DEMANDING HER *ROBES* BACK? WHAT DOES *THAT* MEAN?
YOU SAY HER *EYES* CHANGED, AND THE *COLOR* OF HER HAIR?
SIGH
ALL OF THIS... AYA DOESN'T REMEMBER ANY OF IT, RIGHT?
SHE ALSO YELLED "I WILL WIPE OUT *ALL* THE MIKAGE!" OR SOMESUCH. GOTTA TELL YOU, I THINK SHE *MEANT* IT!
HOW TERRIBLE...
SIGH

Here's volume number 2

Watase here. "Ceres" is safely into its second volume.
This story has a lot of mysteries, so I'm enjoying everyone's "guessing game." I'm sure some of them will become clear in this volume, but it's about to get more and more epic, so my head is spinning already. What am I supposed to do as the number of characters grow?
The one that's popular is actually "Kyō-chan" (Mrs. Q). ☺
Whenever she shows her face, She destroys any serious atmosphere up to that point, so I plan to make her show up often. She's more mysterious in some ways than Tōya. And according to my assistant, "her voice has to be Shigeru Chiba!" ...So since then, I hear Mr. Chiba in my head whenever I write her lines... ☺
I imagine that Aya sounds like Megumi Hayashibara...
The way she's so down to business.
Well, in any case, "Ceres" is based on the "celestial maiden" story, but actually I had another idea as I was about to start a new series. And that was "something that's been overused and needed a fresh twist" according to my editor--"angels and devils." ☺
This concept has become cliché, but I felt challenged to depict it from a different angle... (My editor tells me that another overused concept that we don't need anymore is "the god of death." I think it depends on the way it's depicted.) So my editor was telling me, "something like vampires, except not so common" and I brought up the "celestial maidens" idea that I'd been thinking of. I was secretly plotting that if I draw that "angel story" after having done FY and Ceres, I could call it my **Celestial Trilogy!**
We'll see... Maybe it'll be totally different. The heavenly world might not appear in Ceres at all.

WAIT FOR M...!
OH, NO YOU DON'T!
I'LL JOIN YOU...
I... I'M GOING TO GET SOMETHING TO DRINK.
...DO SOMETHING WITH MY WEIRD POWER AGAIN?
YŪHI, DID I...
DID I WRECK THE HOUSE... AND ATTACK TŌYA...?

DID I HURT MY MOM, TOO?
"DESTROY THE MIKAGES"...?
JUST BEFORE I LOST CONSCIOUSNESS...
...I HEARD A VOICE WITHIN ME:
THIS ALL SEEMS TO BE ABOUT ME, BUT I'M THE ONLY ONE WHO DOESN'T UNDERSTAND ANY OF IT!
YOU JUST... CAME ON TO ME A LITTLE...
N...NO! YOU DIDN'T DO ANYTHING LIKE THAT!
WHY... WHY CAN'T I REMEMBER?!

...EVEN THOUGH I'M *ME,* AND MY BODY IS *MINE!*
I COULDN'T *DO* ANYTHING...
I SUCCUMBED TO THE VOICE OF THE CELESTIAL MAIDEN WITHIN ME.
"RELEASE ME"
DAMMIT...!

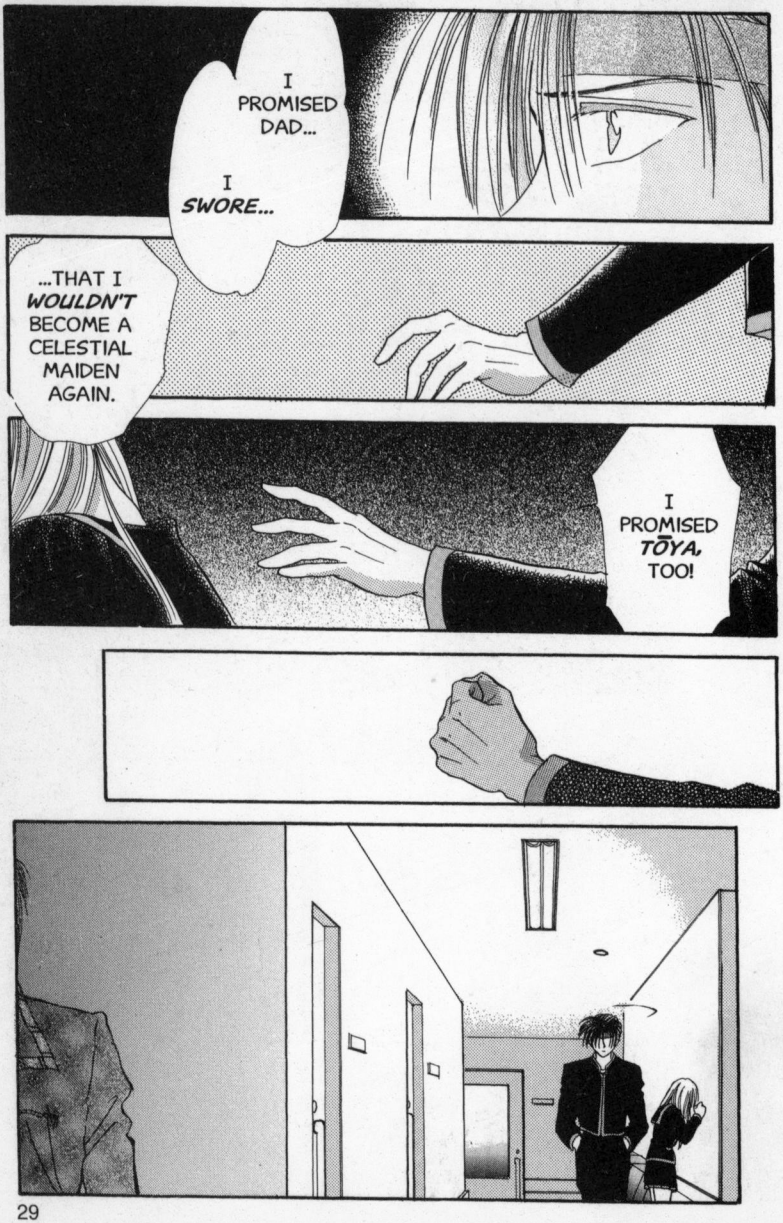
I PROMISED DAD...
I SWORE...
...THAT I WOULDN'T BECOME A CELESTIAL MAIDEN AGAIN.
I PROMISED TŌYA, TOO!

!
IT'S HIM!
HEY!

YOU KEEP HANGING AROUND LIKE SOME KIND OF *STALKER!*
WHAT THE HELL IS *WITH* YOU?
STAY THE HELL *AWAY* FROM AYA, YOU GOT THAT?
I DON'T KNOW HOW *AYA* FEELS ABOUT YOU, BUT TO *ME* YOU'RE JUST A BIG FREAKIN' *EYESORE!*
I'LL PROTECT HER!

DO EVERYTHING *POSSIBLE* TO PROTECT HER...
THEN *PROTECT* HER.
HUFF
HUFF
...FROM THE MIKAGES...
...AND FROM *ME.*
THE CELESTIAL MAIDEN WILL *DESTROY* THE MIKAGES. I HAVE TO HOLD HER BACK SOMEHOW, OR ELSE *EVERYONE* WILL DIE.

AND AKI...?
...BUT TŌYA AND MOM.
NOT JUST GRANDPA...
WAIT FOR ME, AYA.
I'M COMING!
UMPH
UNH...

PA-DAP
I... WON'T LET ANYONE *TOUCH* YOU, AYA.
WE WERE ALWAYS TO-GETHER.
WE...
...SHOULDN'T BE APART. I HAVE TO *REACH* HER, *STAY* WITH HER...

コツ
コツ
コツ
SEARCH FOR HIM! HE COULDN'T HAVE GONE FAR WITH HIS INJURIES!
AYA...
WAIT FOR ME...
AKI'S GONE? WHEN? WHERE?
WHAT WERE YOU DOING? YOU KNOW WHAT YOUR FUTURE WILL BE IF SOMETHING HAPPENS TO HIM...
TŌYA! WHAT TOOK YOU SO LONG?
I'M BEAT. CAN WE TALK LATER?

YOU CAN'T REFUSE, UNLESS YOU'D RATHER *NOT* HAVE YOUR MEMORY BACK.

AKI'S ESCAPED, AND YOU'D BETTER GO *LOOK* FOR HIM. IT'S YOUR *JOB.*
THAT'S RIDICULOUS. YOU SENT ME TO FIND THE SISTER, AND EXPECT ME TO JUST TURN AROUND AND CHASE AFTER HER *BROTHER,* TOO? I NEED A BREAK.
NOT TO MENTION I'M STARVING!

.....
I MET... THE "CELESTIAL MAIDEN."

"WHERE ARE MY... *CELESTIAL ROBES?"*
ANOTHER PERSONALITY EMERGED, HER EYES AND THE COLOR OF HER HAIR CHANGED, AND SHE CALLED HERSELF "CERES."

!!
AS YOU EXPECTED, AYA *TRANS-FORMED.*

CELESTIAL ROBES?
AND...?
NOW I'LL GO LOOK FOR AKI.
THAT'S WHAT YOU *WANT,* ISN'T IT?
I FAILED TO *CAPTURE* HER. THAT'S ALL.
KAGAMI!
DID AKI GO LOOKING FOR *AYA?!*
GRANDFATHER, AKI WILL NEVER FIND AYA.
BUT WHAT HE *MIGHT* FIND... WELL, THAT COULD BE INTERESTING.
CERES... THE CELESTIAL ROBES...

"GOODBYE..."
DAD... MOM...?
WAIT, WHERE ARE YOU GOING?!
"AYA..."
AYA... GOODBYE."
AKI? WAIT FOR ME!
WAIT!

YES?

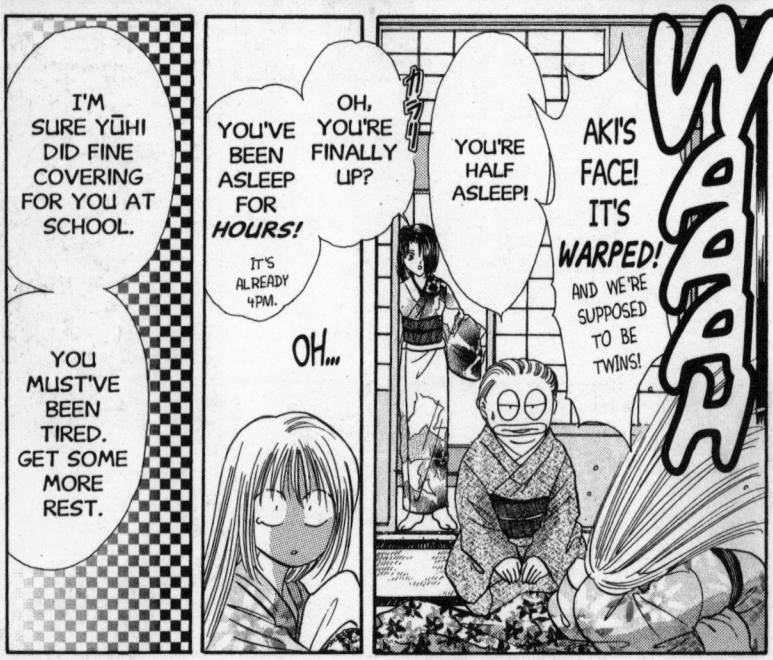
I'M SURE YŪHI DID FINE COVERING FOR YOU AT SCHOOL.
YOU MUST'VE BEEN TIRED. GET SOME MORE REST.
YOU'VE BEEN ASLEEP FOR HOURS!
OH, YOU'RE FINALLY UP?
IT'S ALREADY 4PM.
OH...
YOU'RE HALF ASLEEP!
AKI'S FACE! IT'S WARPED!
AND WE'RE SUPPOSED TO BE TWINS!
WAAAA

SUZUMI! HOW'S MY MOM DOING?
OH YEAH, AFTER WE GOT BACK FROM THE HOSPITAL...
!
S... SUZUMI...
AWW!
YOU'LL GET A JOB AND PAY US BACK, OF COURSE.
SLUMP
NO CHANGE. THEY THINK SHE WAS DRUGGED, BUT THERE'S NO WAY TO BE SURE. WE'LL JUST HAVE TO WAIT.
WHAT DID GRANDPA TELL YOU? WHAT DID THEY DO TO YOU?
MOM ATTACKED ME...
HE WANTED TO STAY HOME THIS MORNING TOO, THE LITTLE WHINER.
AH, IT'S ALMOST TIME FOR YŪHI TO GET HOME.
DON'T WORRY, THE DOCTORS WILL TAKE CARE OF HER. AND WE'LL PAY FOR THE COSTS.

GEEZ, WHAT'S *WITH* THOSE GUYS AT SCHOOL?!
YŪHI WAS...?
HE WAS WORRIED ABOUT *YOU*, REALLY.
YEAH! HI!
WELCOME HOME.
ズサッズカズカ
AYA DOESN'T SHOW UP, SO THEY *HARRASSED* ME ABOUT MY "RUNAWAY WIFE" AND "MARITAL DISPUTES" ...ALL *DAY!*
VACANCY
IT'S NOT LIKE I *MIND* BUT...
MUMBLE!
ANYO

SUZUMI
THERE HE IS.
HOW CLEAR HIS ACTIONS TELL HIS MOOD.
WOULD A BURGLAR TAKE MY UNDERWEAR, TOO?!
WHY ARE YOU ASKING ME? MAYBE IT WAS A BURGLAR.
SHMUP
WHERE'D YOU PUT ALL MY STUFF?!
HEH. YES, MA'AM?
HEH. MRS. Q?

SHOOP
HERE WE GO.
NEXT TO *MY* ROOM?!
OH, RIGHT, AS IF HE'D HAVE THE *GUTS!*
THAT'S RIGHT! HE'LL BE AFTER ME *AHEAD* OF THE MIKAGES!
YOU KNOW...
THIS IS YOUR ROOM FROM NOW ON, YŪHI! CONSIDER IT YOUR *PENANCE* FOR NOT KEEPING AN EYE ON AYA, AND LETTING ALL THIS *HAPPEN!*
YEAH, BUT... THERE'S ONLY A *SLIDING DOOR* BETWEEN US!

GLARE
LISTEN UP! AS LONG AS YOU'RE IN *THIS* HOUSE, YOU'LL DO AS *I* SAY!
OK!
.....
I CAN LISTEN TO *WHATEVER* I WANT IN MY *OWN* ROOM!
TURN THAT *DOWN!*
I'M IN NO MOOD TO LISTEN TO ULFULS.
HEY!
THAT'S *MY* LINE! AND DON'T *YOU* COME BARGING IN HERE JUST BECAUSE YOU HAVE THE *HOTS* FOR ME!
JUST REMEMBER, IF YOU SET ONE FOOT IN MY ROOM AFTER DARK, I'LL *MURDER* YOU!
ARGH!

I'M THE ONE WHO ASKED TO LIVE HERE, SO I CAN'T COMPLAIN.
WHY DON'T YOU LAY IT OUT TO SUZUMI? IF SHE'S YOUR BROTHER'S WIDOW, THEN YOU SHOULD HAVE THE UPPER HAND!
YOU WISH!
BUT... MY BROTHER WAS IN A CAR ACCIDENT SOON AFTER THEY WERE MARRIED.
IT WAS EVEN IN THE NEWSPAPER.
SUZUMI COMES FROM A FAMILY WHO RUNS A SCHOOL IN THE KANSAI REGION. HER FAMILY HAS ALWAYS BEEN CLOSE TO MINE. SHE MARRIED INTO THE AOGIRI FAMILY.
THIS HOUSE IS A BRANCH OF THE MAIN HOUSE, THE AOGIRI SCHOOL OF JAPANESE DANCE. MY BROTHER OPENED IT.

COOKING COMES MORE NATURALLY TO ME.
THEN THERE'S A MAIN SCHOOL? WHAT ABOUT YOU? DON'T *YOU* DANCE?
SHE TOOK OVER AND HAS BEEN RUNNING THIS BRANCH EVER SINCE.
MY MOM WAS A GOOD COOK, BUT SHE DIED WHEN I WAS IN 5TH GRADE. I WASN'T HAPPY WITH ANYONE ELSE'S COOKING, SO I DECIDED TO DO IT MYSELF.
I GUESS I'VE BEEN DOING IT EVER SINCE.
YOU DON'T GET ALONG WITH YOUR STEP-MOTHER?
HE'S HAPPY WITH HIS NEW WIFE. THE SCHOOL WILL BE PASSED ON TO MY OTHER OLDER BROTHER ANYWAY,
SO I'M LIVING HERE...
AND YOUR DAD?

YEAH... I GUESS I'M LUCKY I HAVE A FAMILY I CAN TALK TO.
AKI... I WANT TO SEE HIM...
ANYWAY, YOU AND SUZUMI ARE LIKE *REAL* SIBLINGS.
AKI AND I ARE LIKE THAT, TOO.
.....
FAMILY...
"I DON'T KNOW ANYTHING... ABOUT MY FAMILY, OR MYSELF."
TŌYA... YOU... CAN'T EVEN *TALK* TO ANYONE.
YOU KNOW NOTHING ABOUT YOURSELF... YOU'RE ALONE IN THE WORLD...

SAY...
...YOU KNOW, YOU... UM...
...SHOULD THINK OF *US* AS FAMILY...
カラ…

"YŪHI..."

WHACK
...M!
MM...
SNUFF
URF!
WITH HER INJURED HAND, TOO...
THAT GIRL REALLY MESSES ME UP...
THAT SLIPPED OUT OF MY MOUTH BEFORE I REALIZED IT.
WHAT THE HECK WAS I SAYING?
"I'LL PROTECT AYA."

SHOOT... I'M GETTING LIGHTHEADED.
AND I TOOK OFF WITH NO MONEY...
HUFF
HUFF
HEY!
HE SICK OR SOMETHIN'?
WHAT'S WITH HIM? HE'S IN HIS PAJAMAS.
OUCH!
HOLD IT, PAL!

SHOVE!!
WHAT'D YOU SAY?!
SHUT YOUR FACE AND LET GO OF ME, YOU MORON!
UNH...
SLAM
I SAID LET GO... I DON'T HAVE TIME TO MESS AROUND WITH THE LIKES OF YOU!
WHO YOU CALLIN' A MORON, CREEP?!
YANK
URF!

YEAH, WE'LL ARRANGE IT SO YOU *NEVER* GET OUT OF BED *AGAIN!*
HA HA HA
CHECK TO SEE IF HE HAS ANYTHING *WORTH* ANYTHING.
INVALIDS BELONG IN *BED!*
HMPH!
THIS IS LAME.
UNH!
AYA...
HUH...?

GACK!
EEEUH!
B...BY DOSE...!

.....
AND HERE I THOUGHT I WENT *EASY* ON YOU.
OW... CAREFUL... OW!
THEN GO BACK TO THE MIKAGE HOUSE AND GET BACK IN BED. I'M LOSING *SLEEP* BECAUSE OF YOU.
WHAT'S THE IDEA? I'M *HURT!*
CHOOMP
DON'T MOVE.
AND NOW I'M GOING TO THE AOGIRIS'... TO SEE *AYA!*
I LEFT A LETTER FOR MOM...
NO *WAY* I'M STAYING *THERE* WHEN GRANDPA'S AFTER AYA... AFTER HIS OWN GRANDDAUGHTER'S *LIFE!*

SO YOU'RE WORRIED...
OF COURSE I AM! WE ONLY HAVE EACH OTHER!
I HAVE TO GO TO HER.
SHE'S PRETTY TOUGH, BUT... SHE'S ALSO FRAGILE.
EVEN IN THE STATE YOU'RE IN?
IF I HADN'T BEEN MESSED UP ALREADY, I WOULDN'T HAVE GOTTEN BEAT UP!
OWW...
!
HEY!
OWW...
LET GO!
HEY!
MMM...

Ceres: 2

A little announcement here. **"FY part 2 is going to be an OVA! Six volumes will be released starting in May '97."** There might (?!) be some more events timed to the video releases, so people should keep checking Shōjo Comic comics anthology for info. And I don't know what'll happen just now (Jan. '97), but... **"there might be an FY CD-ROM?!"** --So please keep checking back on that too. Unfortunately, people without a computer are out of luck... They're planning on a digest of all 52 episodes of the TV series and a Q&A corner for the voice actors, among other things... The contents might change (well, if it even gets produced that is).

Oh yeah! For the video of part 2... **I'll be drawing new art for all six video covers!** I think the same art will be used for the LDs... So you'll be able to see Miaka and the seven celestial warriors again. It'll be worth the wait. I'm about to die though...

The novels? ...Huh? ...

Well, so be patient... ☺

× × ×

By the way, I've succeeded in dieting! I lost 8kg (17½ lbs.) in 5 months starting in May '96... And I lost 2 more kg (4 more pounds) but everyone said, "You don't have to get any thinner." So 17½ lbs. it is. Now I eat normally, but I haven't gained the weight back. I have to exercise and get some muscle tone... What I'm most happy about is the feeling of accomplishment, that "I can do it if I try." So I'm a lot thinner than the picture taken for the FY art book (and I even cut and bleached my hair! to brown...) ...So I look like a totally different person. I'd lost weight since the FY event in '96 too...

(JAPANESE FOLK TALES)

One day, as he was passing by a beach, he saw several beautiful celestial maidens bathing in the water. In the pine tree nearby...
...there were magnificent feathered cloaks such as he had never seen. The man realized they belonged to the maidens, and secretly took one home.
The maiden whose robe was taken could not return to heaven. Seeing the man, the maiden became suspicious, asking him, "Have you seen my robes? If you have them, please give them back." But the man feigned ignorance. The maiden, unable to go home, tearfully became the man's wife.
They had children, and many years later, the celestial maiden heard their children singing a nursery rhyme. It told of where the man had hidden the robes.

WHERE ARE WE?
THAT'S THE AOGIRIS'.
AYA'S THERE.
With her robes back, the heavenly maiden returned to the heavenly home she had longed after...
...leaving her husband...
...and her children behind.

TŌYA...
STAY FOR THE NIGHT, BUT THEN COME BACK.
AND... WHEN YOU SEE AYA, SAY NOTHING ABOUT ME.
WHY?
DO YOU KNOW HER?
.....
.....
WELL, THANKS!
CELESTIAL MAIDEN...
...DIDN'T YOU GO BACK TO HEAVEN?

AYA?
AT THIS RATE, I'LL *KILL* ALL MY RELATIVES WITHOUT EVEN *KNOWING* IT. I *CAN'T* GET AKI BACK IF I'M LIKE THIS...
WHY DO YOU *POSSESS* ME?

.....
HUH?
?
AKI...?
AYA...
RUBRUB
O... OH NO! I'M HALLUCI-NATING AGAIN!
...IT'S ME!
ARE YOU OKAY?

!
A...
KI...?
IT'S ALL RIGHT, YŪH!! I LET HIM IN. I TRUST HIM.
HE'S AYA'S TWIN BROTHER...
TWIN?!

LOOK AT YOU... SO...
HAVE YOU LOST *WEIGHT* SINCE OUR BIRTHDAY? YOU ALWAYS *CLAIMED* TO BE ON A DIET BUT...
Y...
YOU BIG *JERK*...
AKI!!

YŪHI.
NOW'S YOUR CHANCE TO SHOW OFF YOUR *SKILL*. WHIP UP A FEAST FIT FOR THE OCCASION.
.....
YEAH.
I THOUGHT... I'D *NEVER* SEE YOU AGAIN!
I *WORRIED* ABOUT YOU EVERY DAY!
Y...YOU DON'T KNOW HOW I *FELT*... SO ALONE, ABAN-DONED...

TŌYA? *TŌYA* BROUGHT AKI HERE...?

EEW! NO!

SUDDENLY I'M IN NO MOOD TO COOK. HOW ABOUT A ROUND OF INSTANT RAMEN?

NO WONDER YOU WERE DOWN SO LONG!
ARE YOU SURE YOU'RE OK NOW?
YEAH! IT LOOKS A LOT WORSE THAN IT FEELS. I'M FINE!
AND THAT TERRIFIC MEAL YOU MADE HAS RESTORED ME A LOT!
WHAT? REALLY?! WELL, HEY, I COULDN'T AGREE MORE!
.....
WOW...
...ALL THOSE WOUNDS...
MAN, THEY LOOK PAINFUL.
AND THANK YOU... FOR TAKING CARE OF AYA.

N...NO!
ARE YOU SURE YOU DON'T KNOW WHAT'S GOING ON, WHY GRANDPA IS AFTER YOU...?
DARNED IF I KNOW WHY ALL THIS HAPPENED, AYA.
!
WELL, I'LL LEAVE YOU TWO TO REST UP. IT'S BEEN A WHILE SINCE YOU'VE HAD TIME ALONE.
I'LL BE NEXT DOOR, SO JUST HOLLER IF YOU WANT SOMETHING.
G'NIGHT!
G'NIGHT.
I CAN'T TELL HIM...
SAY, AKI, LET'S HOLD HANDS.
HM...? OH, OK.

IT'S LIKE BEING LITTLE AGAIN. IT MAKES ME FEEL SO *SAFE*...
YEAH, I GUESS IT DOES...

HEY, AKI... YOU'RE STILL THE SAME AKI, RIGHT?
HA HA... ...OF COURSE.
OH! OH YEAH, AKI, THE EAR-RINGS...
I'LL *STAY* WITH YOU, AYA, DON'T WORRY. NOW GO TO SLEEP.
GOOD NIGHT...

!!
UGH!
I'VE FOUND YOU!
THOSE WOUNDS ON YOUR BODY... YOU ARE THE MAN WHO SHAMED ME!!
RETURN THEM! RETURN MY CELESTIAL ROBES!!

...UNH...
SO... STRONG...!!
MY CELESTIAL ROBES! GIVE THEM BACK, OR...
P... PASSING OUT...

TŌYA...
YOU AGAIN!
COME ON, AKI... THIS WAY.
...!

HEY, WHAT HAP...
!!
...!...
TH... THOSE CLOTHES...
AYA?!
GET OUT OF THE WAY, TŌYA.
THAT MAN IS MY NEMESIS.
LISTEN, AKI, THAT'S NOT YOUR TWIN SISTER RIGHT NOW. GET OUTSIDE.
!!

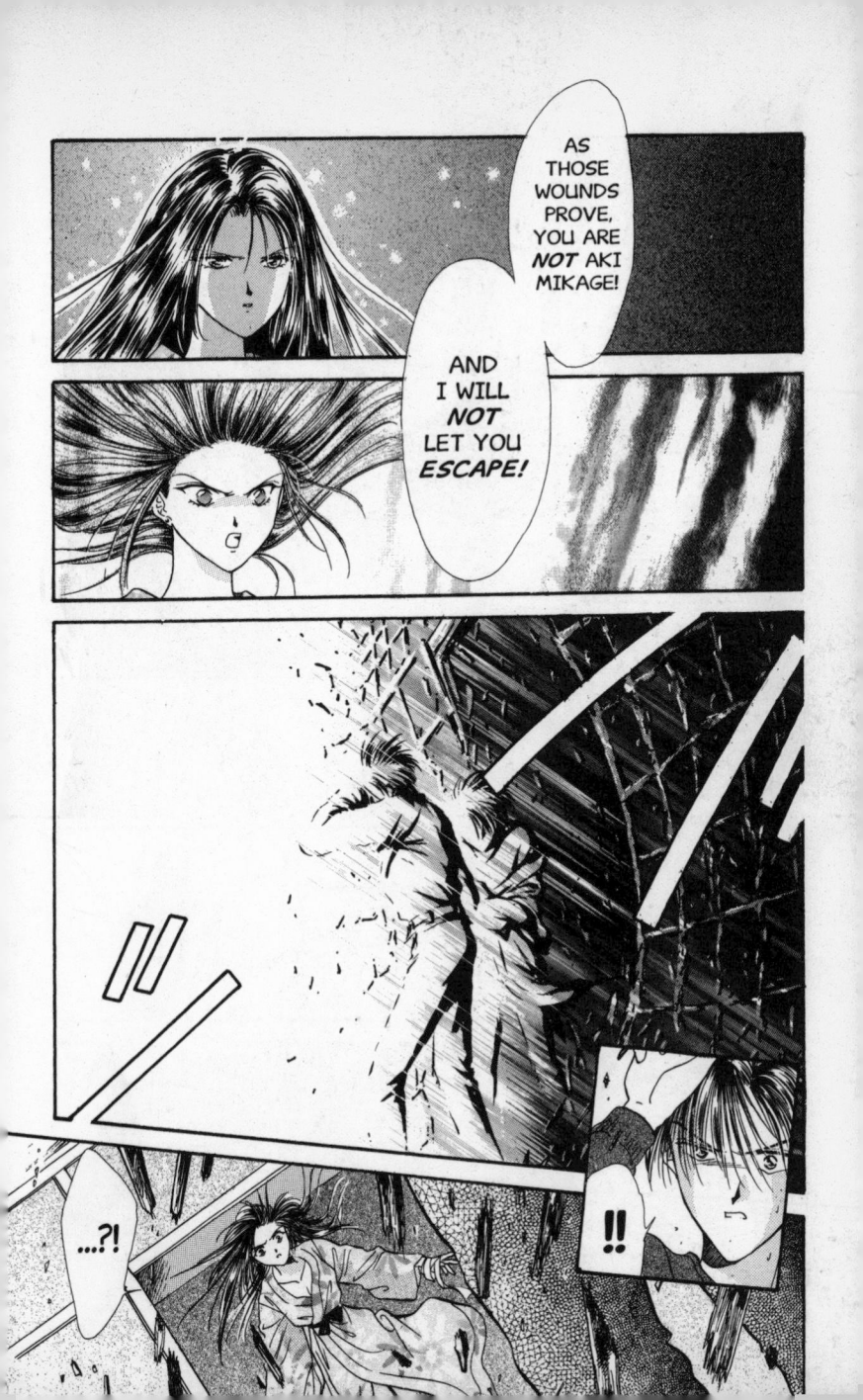
AS THOSE WOUNDS PROVE, YOU ARE *NOT* AKI MIKAGE!
AND I WILL *NOT* LET YOU *ESCAPE!*
!!
...?!

Yuhi
THAT'S NOT MY WORRY. I'M HERE TO PROTECT AKI, THAT'S ALL.
YOU ARE UNAFFECTED, AS BEFORE.
WHY DON'T MY POWERS WORK ON YOU?!
!!
AYA!

WHAT'S HAPPENED TO YOU, AYA?!
GET A HOLD OF YOURSELF! IT'S ME!! WE'RE FINALLY... FINALLY BACK TOGETHER...
AYA!!
DON'T...
...TOUCH ME!

UNH!
CERES! YOU SAID AKI IS YOUR NEMESIS...
THAT HE MUST RETURN YOUR... CELESTIAL ROBES. WHAT'S THAT ALL ABOUT?
WHEN I FIRST... CAME DOWN FROM HEAVEN... THAT MAN...
...MIKAGE... STOLE THE CELESTIAL ROBES FROM ME...
BECAUSE OF THAT, I COULD NEVER GO HOME... AND HE FORCED ME...
SEE THOSE WOUNDS? THEY'RE THE ONES I LASHED INTO HIM WITH MY POWERS....!!
!

I'M... THAT MAN? I...IT'S NOT TRUE!
IT CAN'T BE TRUE...
YOU HEARD HER!! CERES IS GOING TO KILL AKI!
GET AYA BACK!! GET HER BACK, NOW!!
!!
IT IS! ONLY YOU KNOW WHERE MY CELESTIAL ROBES ARE. RETURN THEM, BEFORE I...
YŪHI!!
I'M AKI, AND YOU'RE MY LITTLE SISTER, AYA...
HONEST, I DON'T KNOW ANYTHING ABOUT THESE CELESTIAL ROBES!
I VOWED REVENGE, AND I SHALL HAVE IT!
I'LL RECLAIM MY CELESTIAL ROBES AND DESTROY THE MIKAGES!

I AM NO SUCH THING TO YOU! YOU ARE MY ENEMY!! ALL THE MIKAGES ARE MY...
YŪKI...!!
NO! I WILL NOT GO BACK!! AYA WILL SLEEP UNTIL I'M FINISHED... WITH EVERY-THING!!
THAT'S FAR ENOUGH, CERES! TIME TO GO BACK!
NOW... AKI! LET'S GET OUT OF HERE.
!!
I MEAN IT! DO YOU WANT TO FIGHT YOUR SISTER?

!!
DAMMIT! THERE'S NO OTHER WAY...
A-H!
STOP!!
OOH!

AKI...
HEY YOU GUYS!
...TŌYA?!
WHAT THE...? THE DOOR'S SHATTERED!
I COULDN'T HAVE...?
TŌYA! WHERE ARE YOU TAKING AKI?!
AYA!!

KA-KA
TŌYA!
HEY, WAIT A SECOND!
HUFF HUFF

THANK YOU FOR YOUR EFFORTS, TŌYA.
KAGAMI...
WE'LL TAKE IT FROM HERE. AKI, GET IN MY CAR.

♦ Yūhi ♦

Oh, recently I got hooked on a certain food! ...And that's "**natto**" (a fermented soybean treat)!! My family proved wrong the whole theory that "Kansai people (western Japan) don't eat much natto," and had it all the time. I was the only one among them who winced at the smell, but that's now a distant memory...

I'm pretty fussy about my food, but I was listening to the people on TV extol natto's virtues--it's nutritious; it's good for the brain; and it fights bad bacteria--one good thing after another! I thought, "I gotta try this!" So I made it more palatable by using the mustard that comes with it, and when you add shiso (Japanese basil) dressing (adding vinegar is good too. *Oh! add red pepper! and scallions!*)

It's soooo good!

I got so hooked that I get depressed if I don't eat it every morning. I could eat it three times a day! Nowadays I can eat it without the mustard or anything! I never thought such a delicacy existed... (Okay, I'm exaggerating.)

I guess as you get older, your tastes, including the foods you like, change. I don't like fried and greasy foods anymore, for example.

Aside from food, other things like the way I think are changing a lot these days. I get irritable a lot lately, and there's all this defiance welling up inside me. Then one of my acquaintances said, "That means you're trying to break out of your previous shell," "Your ego is growing," and so forth. "It's like that when teenagers become delinquent." ...What?! Does that mean that I'm going to be a delinquent at **my** age?! ...But I hear that it happens even to people in their 30's.

WHERE IS HE?! WHY DID YOU TAKE HIM? DIDN'T YOU BRING HIM HERE?!
SO... YOU'RE BACK.
AS FOR AKI, KAGAMI TOOK HIM AWAY IN THAT CAR.
!!
YOUR GRAND-FATHER WILL PROBABLY LOCK HIM UP FOR GOOD THIS TIME.
YOU SAID "YOU'RE BACK."
...YOU MEAN I BECAME THE HEAVENLY MAIDEN AGAIN?
DID I? AND DID I ATTACK AKI? AND YOU?!
ANSWER ME! NOBODY EVER TELLS ME ANYTHING!!

...DO SOMETHING ABOUT YOUR *CLOTHES* FIRST.
DON'T BE RIDICULOUS. AND *LOWER* YOUR VOICE. IT'S THE MIDDLE OF THE NIGHT.
AND YOU'RE NO *DIFFERENT!* I BET YOU KNOW *EVERYTHING,* DON'T YOU? THAT REALLY *PISSES* ME *OFF!!*
I'M NOT LETTING YOU GO UNTIL YOU *TELL* ME!
YOU MIGHT...
!
IF YOU INSIST ON TAGGING ALONG, BE MY GUEST. MY CAR'S RIGHT OVER THERE.
I'M THE ONE THEY'LL *ARREST* IF ANYONE SEES US LIKE THIS, SO I'M *OUTTA* HERE.

YEAH, WELL, HOW FAR DID SHE CHASE THOSE GUYS, I WONDER?
DAMMIT, SHE MOVES FAST!
KNOCKING YOU COLD GAVE HER A BIT OF A HEAD START.
AYA?!

WHAT I FIND REALLY WEIRD IS THAT YOU BROUGHT HER BACK WITH A KI...
DON'T SAY IT! IT'S EMBARRASSING!
.....
I WONDER ABOUT CERES...SHE'S NOT WHAT I IMAGINED AT ALL.
AND IF WHAT SHE SAID IS TRUE, THEN WE HAVE A BIG PROBLEM.

SAY WHAT?!
OH.
I'M GOING HOME. THE WORKDAY IS LONG OVER.
MY CONDO.
HEY! WHERE ARE WE GOING?
BET YOU DON'T EVEN HAVE A DRIVER'S LICENSE.
REMEMBER, YOU INSISTED ON COMING ALONG.
.....
COME IN.

OH...
TAKE A SHOWER FIRST. I'D RATHER YOU DIDN'T WANDER AROUND WITH *DIRTY* FEET AND CLOTHES.
WHAT'S THE MATTER? AFRAID OF HOT WATER? OR *ME?*
GLARE
HMPH! AS *IF!*
FEEL FREE TO USE THE TOWELS AND THE WASHING MACHINE.
IT'S *YOUR* COUSIN KAGAMI WHO GOT ME THIS PLACE, AFTER ALL.
!
TAKE YOUR TIME.
SHEESH, WHY DID I FOLLOW HIM?
I *KNOW* THERE'S NO POINT IN LISTENING TO *ANYTHING* HE HAS TO SAY.

IT'S ALL HAPPENING *WITHIN* ME.
BUT I BELONG TO *ME.* MY BODY AND MY WILL AND MY HEART...
AYA MIKAGE... YOUR *LIFE* IS YOUR OWN, RIGHT...?
カチャ...
!
ASLEEP ALREADY.
IT'S COLD.

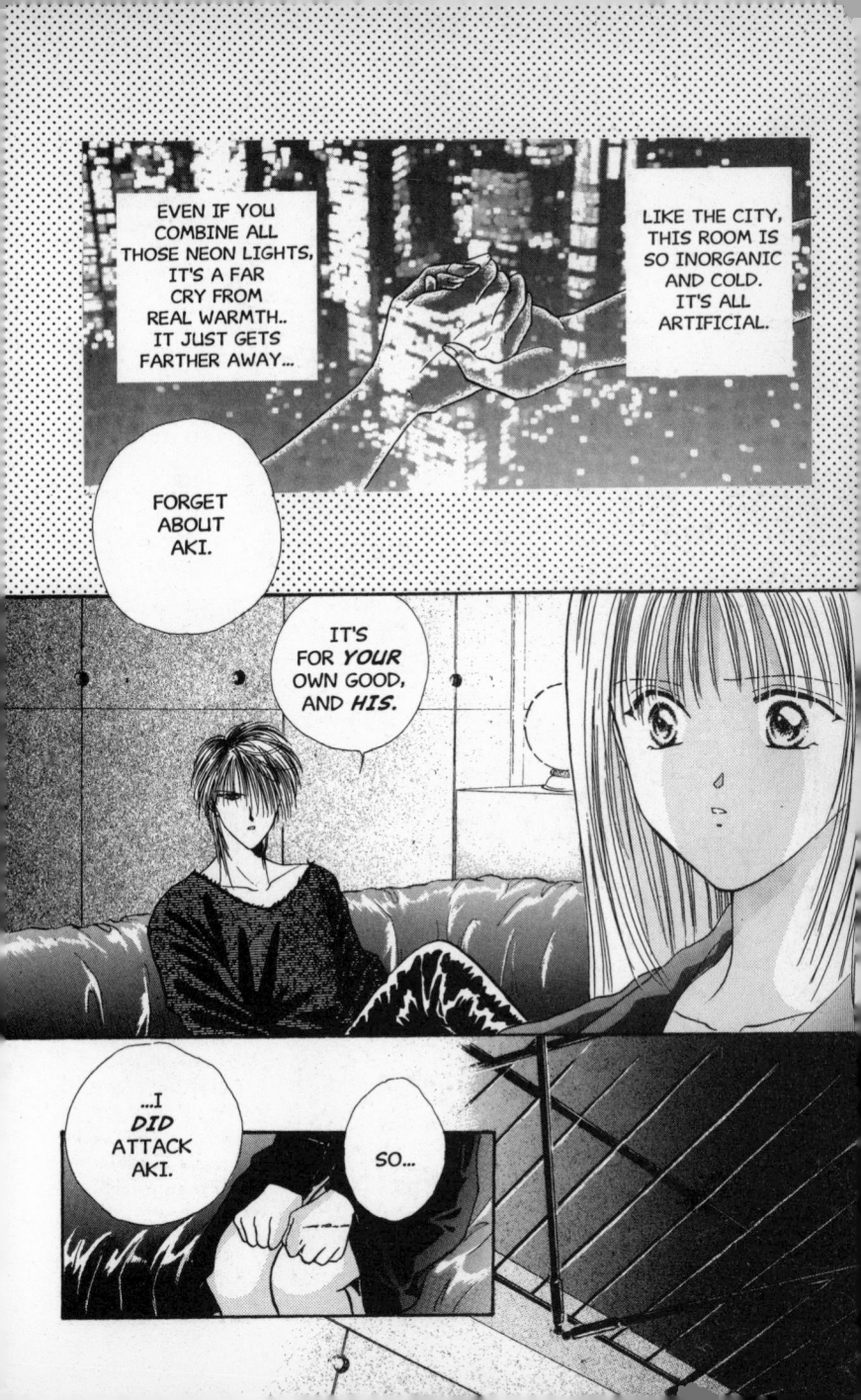
EVEN IF YOU COMBINE ALL THOSE NEON LIGHTS, IT'S A FAR CRY FROM REAL WARMTH.. IT JUST GETS FARTHER AWAY...
LIKE THE CITY, THIS ROOM IS SO INORGANIC AND COLD. IT'S ALL ARTIFICIAL.
FORGET ABOUT AKI.
IT'S FOR *YOUR* OWN GOOD, AND *HIS.*
...I *DID* ATTACK AKI.
SO...

GIMME A BREAK, TELL ME WHY...
...WHY ME AND AKI?!
IT'S PROBABLY "FATE"...
"FATE?" WHAT DO YOU MEAN?
WHO SAYS IT'S "FATE?"
WHY DOES "FATE" GET TO DECIDE ALL THIS, WITHOUT CONSULTING US?
AND THAT'S SUPPOSED TO MEAN WE HAVE TO GIVE UP? WE CAN ONLY PISS AND MOAN WHEN FACED WITH "FATE?!"

YOU TAKE THE BED. I'LL DRIVE YOU BACK TO THE AOGIRIS IN THE MORNING.
THERE'S NOTHING ELSE I CAN TELL YOU.
...THAT YOU AND I ARE ENEMIES?
...IT IS "FATE"...
THEN...
.....
YOU'RE SHIVERING...?

SHUM
OH! IT'S NOTHING!
I'M COLD.
THAT'S THE BED, RIGHT? I'LL TURN IN, THEN.
I CAN'T TELL IF I'M SHIVERING FROM THE COLD OR... IS IT ANGER? SADNESS?
BUT ARE THESE MY FEELINGS?
OR...
...ARE THEY MY OTHER...

HEY!!
WH... WHAT ARE YOU DOING?!
YOU'RE COLD...
I'M GOING TO STAY LIKE THIS UNTIL YOU STOP SHIVERING.
BUT IF YOU DON'T LIKE IT, PUSH ME AWAY. YOU DECIDE.
.....
BUT... WHAT IF I TRANS-FORM AGAIN?
I'D END UP KILLING YOU!

I'LL DEAL WITH THAT... WHEN IT HAPPENS.
SHIVER
WHAT'S *THAT* MEAN? WHY'D YOU SAY THAT?
DON'T GET SO CLOSE... OR I WON'T BE ABLE TO STAY RATIONAL! OH, YOU'RE NOT BEING *FAIR...!*
OF COURSE I CAN'T PUSH YOU AWAY... OF COURSE I CAN'T *KILL* YOU!!
FOR NOW, WHATEVER THE REASON, I JUST WANT TO KEEP HOLDING YOU.
THIS I KNOW FOR SURE...

NOT THE MIKAGES...
...AND NOT AKI.
THE ONE I HAVE TO FIGHT ISN'T TŌYA...
...LOVE YOU...!
...I...
...JUST LIKE THIS, FOREVER!
PLEASE HOLD ME...
IT'S THE OTHER ME... CERES...

...FOR AKI'S SAKE...
YEAH...
...WITH MYSELF...
I'LL *FIGHT* IT, I SWEAR...
...AND TO *PROTECT* THIS LOVE.

SAY...
HAVE YOU ALWAYS BEEN ALONE LIKE THIS? CAN YOU REMEMBER WHEN YOU LOST YOUR MEMORY?
HM...
YES, IT WAS... TWO OR THREE MONTHS AGO.

I TRIED HARD TO RETRACE MY MEMORY, BUT ALL THAT CAME TO ME WERE TWO NAMES: "TŌYA" AND "MIKAGE."
AND ALL I HAD ON ME WAS A COUPLE HUNDRED DOLLARS IN CASH.
I HAD NO MEMORY OF WHAT HAPPENED, WHO I WAS, WHERE I LIVED, ANYTHING.
WHAT I DO REMEMBER, I CAME TO LYING IN A PARK IN THE RAIN...
I WAS CONTRACTED AS A BODYGUARD, BUT I WAS GIVEN A BONUS AND A CAR AND THIS CONDO...
SO YOU FOUND MY FAMILY? AND THEY GOT YOU TO WORK FOR THEM IN EXCHANGE FOR GETTING YOUR MEMORY BACK?
THEY'RE REALLY WOUND UP ABOUT THIS "CELESTIAL MAIDEN" THING.
...ONCE THEY FOUND OUT I COULD *WITHSTAND* YOUR... THE CELESTIAL MAIDEN'S *POWERS.*

.....
PROTECTING AKI AND FIGHTING ME IS JUST DOING WHAT MY FAMILY... WHAT MR. KAGAMI REQUIRES?
.....
I SEE...
I DON'T KNOW.
YOU AND AKI... HAVE SOMETHING I'M NOT FAMILIAR WITH.
I DON'T HAVE A DESPERATE, PERSONAL INTEREST IN PROTECTING ANYTHING. I DON'T *LOVE* ANYONE, I DON'T *HATE* ANYONE.
BUT WATCHING YOU AND YOUR BROTHER...
...MADE ME FEEL LIKE I'VE LOST SOMETHING BEYOND MEMORIES, SOMETHING *IMPORTANT*...
THEN...

I CAN'T BRING BACK YOUR MEMORY, BUT I CAN TEACH YOU HOW TO HAVE SOME FUN!
EVEN IF YOU CAN'T FIGURE OUT YOUR FEELINGS NOW, RELAX AND GET TO LIKE ME!
...GO OUT WITH ME!
LIKE DOING KARAOKE AND GOING OUT TO PARTIES!
ARE YOU... IN A POSITION TO TALK ABOUT SUCH FRIVOLOUS THINGS?
I'M NOT FRIVOLOUS, I'M SERIOUS!
HUH?

I TOLD YOU THAT I LOVE YOU, SO BE A MAN AND ANSWER ME!
GIRLS ARE ALWAYS SERIOUS ABOUT LOVE!
YEAH... SO GO TO SLEEP...
REALLY? FOR REAL?!
ALL RIGHT, I'LL THINK ABOUT IT...
HEH.
...GEEZ.
OKAY, CERES... CAN YOU HEAR ME?
YOU DON'T GIVE UP, DO YOU...

Ceres: 2

...Yeah, these days I'm feeling kinda rebellious. I guess it happens even in your 20's. I feel it toward my work, too -- I feel like I just want to destroy everything I've made up to now. Before, it was all about love and hope.
All candy-coated and sugary sweet, and looking at it now, it feels kinda, "Blech," or something. Well, my personality's pretty much the same as it's always been, but I honestly feel that way. Putting it in Ceres-related terms, it's probably because Ceres, a facet of the main character Aya, is someone from the dark side. She feels within her that, "Love and dreams and wimpy crap like that are only a fantasy," (though I'm sure she's not that vulgar). I think Aya's gotten the worst treatment I've ever doled out in any of my works. Her relatives are her enemies, and even the other self within her is an enemy of sorts! Once you step into the dark side of the world, you get really caught up in it. The Aogiri family isn't so dark though... Tōya also has a bit of a rule-breaker side. I won't let Tōya have any lovey-dovey, cutesy, sugary-sweet love! He's more suited to straight-black coffee love... After all, he projects an image that suggests a guy who would look good covered in blood. I think I'll let him do that some time. SCARED? On the other hand, the straightforward, transparent type is Yūhi, so I'll be happy if he goes at it with a half-chipper, half-serious attitude. But I'm sure Tōya will be amazing when he actually does it.
...DOES WHAT?

I'VE NEVER PULLED AN ALL-NIGHTER, EVEN FOR EXAMS.
WHY... AM I DOING THIS FOR HER...
EEYUGH... I OUGHTA SKIP SCHOOL TODAY.
IT'S SATURDAY ANYWAY, AIN'T IT?
BLEAH
THAT IDIOT.
SHE NEVER CAME HOME...
HELLOOO?
OH... YŪHI...?
"SORRY?" "SORRY" DOESN'T CUT IT! I'VE BEEN LOOKING ALL OVER FOR YOU!
S...SORRY THAT I... DIDN'T CALL...
AYA?!

ALONE WITH HIM...
MORNING AFTER...
SPENT THE NIGHT...

SORRY TO CAUSE SO MUCH CONCERN. I'LL DRIVE AYA BACK.

I'M REALLY SORRY ABOUT THAT. I DIDN'T MEAN TO CAUSE TROUBLE AGAIN.
NO KIDDING!
SIGH... HE'S SERIOUSLY PISSED OFF...

WHERE ARE YOU NOW?!
HEY, AOGIRI?

YOU BASTARD!

I'LL COME GET HER MYSELF! WHAT'S THE ADDRESS?
NO WAY ARE YOU DRIVING HER HOME!

YOU HEAR THAT?
HEY! ANSWER ME!
HANG UP!
MRS. Q!
OOOOG...
MRS. Q, GET THE CAR! I FOUND OUT WHERE AYA IS, AND WE'RE GOING TO GO GET HER!
YOU FOUND AYA?!
KNOCK IT OFF!
SNUGGLE
OH, YŪHI, YOU SHOULDN'T SNEAK INTO A LADY'S BEDROOM LIKE THIS!

.....
GEEZ, MRS. Q! YOU'RE SOOO NOT A MORNING PERSON!
CHUCKLE...
HE'S SO TRANSPARENT.
I'M GOING TO FILLET THAT SKIRT CHASER TŌYA AND SERVE HIM SASHIMI-STYLE... MAYBE GRILLED!
AND YOU'RE GOING AFTER HER? BUT WHY ARE YOU IN YOUR COOKING GETUP?
WE'RE OFF!
WITH THE FIRE HE'S GOT LIT UNDER HIM, PROBABLY SOONER.
I GUESS HE'LL GET HERE IN ABOUT 20 MINUTES.
WE CAN BE ALONE TOGETHER... ONLY A LITTLE WHILE LONGER...

HM?
.....
THEN HE'LL PUT THAT COLLAR WITH THE MIKAGE FAMILY SEAL AROUND HIS NECK AGAIN...
!!
H... HEY...
.....

A HICKEY?
DOESN'T THAT USUALLY WORK THE OTHER WAY AROUND, THE GUY GIVING...? ANYWAY, IT'LL DISAPPEAR IN A DAY OR TWO...
THEN YOU'LL HAVE TO COME SEE ME AGAIN...
HEH HEH...
THAT'S MY SEAL!
SO YOU DON'T FORGET WHAT WE TALKED ABOUT LAST NIGHT!
?
MUMBLE...
YEAH... IF I COULD GO OUT WITH YOU... I'M SURE IT WOULD BE FUN...
CHUCKLE...
YOU'RE WEIRD.
...AND I'LL MAKE ANOTHER ONE!

HUH...?
...SO THAT YOU CAN *STAY* JUST THE WAY YOU ARE NOW.
THIS... IS *MY* SEAL.

MAY IT HELP YOU *WIN* THE FIGHT FOR YOUR-SELF.
THEN...
THEN...?
HELLO.
OH...
IT'S ME.
GOOD JOB LAST NIGHT, TŌYA.
I NEED TO TALK TO YOU ABOUT AKI, NOW.
RRRRRR

RIGHT NOW?
BUT...
...SURE. I'LL HEAD OVER IN A BIT.
LATER...
WAS THAT KAGAMI?!
...
DINGDONG DINGDONG DINGDONG DINGDONG
HEY AYA!
MRS. Q, YOU CAN STOP DRIVING NOW! WE'RE HERE!
GEEZ, GET A GRIP!
JUST 'ROUND THE NEXT CORNER...
IS THAT ALL YOU'VE GOT TO SAY AFTER WORRYING EVERYONE SICK?!
BE QUIET, YOU!

WHO'S DAMAGED GOODS?!
BOO!
HEY, ARE YOU TRYING TO DUCK OUT ON YOUR RESPONSIBILITIES? YOU'VE TURNED AYA INTO DAMAGED GOODS, YOU BASTARD!
GUESS WE'LL SPLIT HERE.
!!
GREAT! I WASTED ALL THAT ENERGY GETTING PISSED OFF.
MUMBLE GRUMBLE...
WELL, IT'S NOT LIKE I WAS WORRIED OR ANYTHING.
.....
NOT ONLY ARE YOU MAKING STUPID ASSUMPTIONS, YOU'RE YELLING THEM AT THE TOP OF YOUR LUNGS!
WHAT? YOU MEAN... NOTHING HAPPENED?
NOTHING LIKE THAT!

HUH?! HEY! DON'T YOU DRIVE OFF WITHOUT ME!
ANYWAY, LET'S GO HOME!
GO HOME YOURSELF!
YOU THINK YOU SHOULD BE CHASING THIS GUY'S ASS RIGHT NOW? WHAT ABOUT AKI? WHERE IS HE?
HEH. FRET NOT! I'M AN EXPERT AT STALKING!
CAREFUL, MRS. Q. MAKE SURE HE DOESN'T SEE YOU!

AKI WAS *TAKEN* AGAIN...BY MY COUSIN. TŌYA IS GOING TO MEET HIM NOW.
SO... YOU FOLLOW HIM. THEN WHAT?
I DON'T KNOW...
BUT...
...I'VE SURE GOT A *LOT* OF THINGS TO SAY TO *KAGAMI.*
JUST A MOMENT. THE COMPUTER WILL SCAN YOUR FACE AND AUTOMATICALLY OPEN THE DOOR.

NOTHING.
WHAT'S THE MATTER?
CHUCKLE
PRRRR

DOES IT HAVE SOMETHING TO DO WITH THE CURRENT PROJECT...?
WHY ARE YOU KEEPING AKI AT THE OFFICE?
NICE TIMING. HIS BODYGUARD IS HEADING THAT WAY NOW.
YES, BUT JUST AKI IS NOT ENOUGH.
WHAT IS IT?
BOSS, AKI IS AWAKE.
WHAT'S THE MATTER?
AYA...?!
THE OTHER ONE... HIS OTHER HALF...
?!

THAT OTHER HALF HAS JUST ARRIVED.
LET'S INVITE HER IN.
MAN, WHAT AN EDIFICE! YOUR FAMILY MUST BE FILTHY RICH!
WOULDN'T KNOW BY ME! MY IMMEDIATE FAMILY WAS AVERAGE, STRICTLY MIDDLE CLASS. THE MONEY'S WITH MY OTHER RELATIVES.
WELL... I JUST CAN'T FIGURE OUT THE CORPORATE WORLD. IT'S TOO STRANGE. AN OFFICE BUILDING IS LIKE AN RPG DUNGEON, AND I CAN'T IMAGINE WHAT GOES ON INSIDE.
IT'S LIKE ALL THOSE ADULTS ARE THE WARRIORS AND MONSTERS ALL JUMBLED TOGETHER, FIGHTING ECONOMIC WAR DAY IN AND DAY OUT.
AM I GOING TO JOIN A WORLD LIKE THIS ONE DAY?
SIGH THE VERY THOUGHT IS A BORE!
OH NO, I'VE LOST TŌYA.
IT'S THE WEEKEND... ALL ENTRANCES ARE CLOSED...

YEESH! DON'T *DO* THAT!
HUMPA HUMPA HUMPA
GYACK!
AYA! YOU FOUND AN *ENTRANCE?*
YŪ...
EXCUSE ME!
DID TŌYA COME THROUGH HERE TOO?

YŪHI...
!!
HEY!
OPEN UP! AYA!
.....

I CAN'T HEAR YOU! WHAT...?!
HEY! WHERE ARE YOU GOING?!
BLINK
I'M JUST GOING TO CHECK IT OUT!
HANG ON, YŪH!!
TŌYA?!
BLINK
SHUUSH
VRRRRR
I'VE COME THIS FAR... CAN'T TURN BACK NOW!

HELLO, AYA.
I'M YOUR COUSIN...
GRANDFATHER'S OUT TO KILL YOU, BUT I'M NOT GRANDFATHER.
WAIT A SECOND.
HEH! WRONG FLOOR! BYE!

AND CUT THE "COUSIN" CRAP! IT REALLY PISSES ME OFF!
TALK? DON'T MAKE ME LAUGH.
SOMEPLACE WE CAN TALK WITHOUT INTER-RUPTION.
WHAT'S THIS?
WHAT DID YOU DO TO MY MOM?!
WHO KILLED MY FATHER?!
AH, BUT AREN'T YOU THE ONE WHO THREATENS TO DO SOMETHING TO AKI...
...IF YOU DO ANYTHING TO AKI ON TOP OF ALL THAT, I'LL MAKE SURE YOU REGRET IT! I'LL GO TO THE COPS AND...
AND TŌYA... YOU'RE TAKING ADVANTAGE OF HIS MEMORY LOSS!

....CERES?
WHAT DO YOU MEAN...? I'M *AYA!*
NOT ALWAYS. YOU TRANSFORM...
I WON'T *ANYMORE!* I *WON'T* LET HER OUT!
I SEE. THEN WHAT *SHOULD* I DO?
YES, QUITE THE "MODERN TEENAGER," AREN'T YOU?
HMPH.
THEN I WON'T HAVE TO TREAT YOU LIKE A KID...

WHA...
!!!
TO START, I WON'T LET YOU *OUT* OF HERE...
THERE'RE THINGS I MUST *KNOW*, MUCH I MUST *TEST*.
...UNTIL *CERES* APPEARS!

BIRTHDAY: Unknown (estimated age 20-24)

BLOODTYPE: AB (confirmed by lab results)

HEIGHT: 184cm (6') all other statistics unknown

Above average intelligence, athletics, and muscular strength, but lacking in emotional expression.

TŌYA

DAMN!
ACCESS MUST BE KEYED TO THE FACES OF EMPLOYEES AND RELATIVES!
YŪHI! WHERE'S AYA?
MRS. Q...
A CAMERA...
DAMMIT, OPEN UP!
THIS IS A MIGHTY "CONVENIENT" SECURITY SYSTEM, THAT ONLY LETS AYA IN!

PBBTH
HM?
PLEASE GOD, TELL ME!
WELL, I DON'T GET IT, BUT I'M GLAD YOU WERE HERE, MRS. Q.
I DON'T UNDERSTAND EITHER, BUT I'M GLAD I WAS OF SOME USE.
ALL RIGHT! LET'S GO AFTER AYA!
BUT WHY?!
WE'RE IN.
THERE ARE ABOUT 50 FLOORS. WHERE SHALL WE START...?
.....

IT'S NO USE. THE DOOR IS CONTROLLED BY THE COMPUTER, AND THERE ARE NO WINDOWS. THIS ROOM IS COMPLETELY SEALED.
!!

WH-WHAT ARE YOU GONNA *DO?!* WE'RE *COUSINS!*

IF YOU DON'T WANT TO GET HURT, LET CERES OUT.
IT'S ALSO SOUNDPROOF. OF COURSE, BEING A HOLIDAY, THERE'S NOBODY AROUND TO HEAR ANYTHING ANYWAY.

WHY...?
THEY PROBABLY DIDN'T WANT ANY STRANGERS SULLYING THE *PURITY* OF THE PRECIOUS "CELESTIAL MAIDEN" BLOODLINE.

YOU *DIDN'T* KNOW?
YOUR MOM IS YOUR DAD'S SECOND COUSIN.

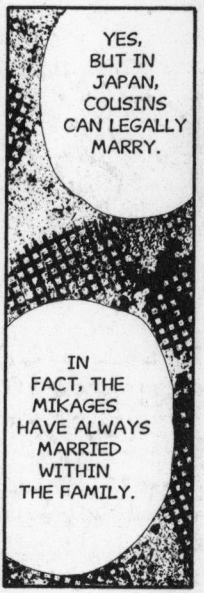
YES, BUT IN JAPAN, COUSINS CAN LEGALLY MARRY.
IN FACT, THE MIKAGES HAVE ALWAYS MARRIED WITHIN THE FAMILY.

"ALWAYS," HUH? WHAT A PAIN IN THE ASS FOR *US*, THE DESCENDANTS!
REALLY? FOR MYSELF, I'M *GLAD!*
I COULD MEET THE CELESTIAL MAIDEN, REBORN INTO THE MODERN WORLD...
GAH!
PBBT!

RELEASE HER! LET CERES OUT.
LEMME GO!
IDIOT!
!!
.....
!!

NO!
!
YES, THAT'S IT.
AH, SO STUBBORN. IT SEEMS YOU HAVEN'T HAD ENOUGH.
SHALL WE GO A LITTLE *FURTHER,* THEN...?

TŌYA? ...WHAT ARE YOU DOING HERE?
AKI?
NO! I *MUST* HOLD CERES BACK!
I... DON'T KNOW. THEY BROUGHT ME HERE IN THE MIDDLE OF THE NIGHT.
WEREN'T *YOU* AT YOUR *GRAND-FATHER'S...?*
I WAS CALLED OVER BY KAGAMI.
WELL, THEY TOLD ME TO MAKE MYSELF AT HOME... KAGAMI'S DAD... HE'S THE COMPANY'S PRESIDENT... IS MY UNCLE, AFTER ALL.
I HAD NO IDEA THERE WAS A RESIDENTIAL COMPLEX ON THE 10TH FLOOR OF THE HIGH-RISE.

AS IF I CARED. I'M *SICK* OF THE WHOLE THING.
BUT NOW I UNDERSTAND WHY THEY'D WANT TO DO AWAY WITH AYA. THEY DON'T WANT TO BE RUINED...
AND MY GRANDFATHER IS THE CHAIRMAN... ALL IN ALL, THEY RUN A *HUGE* COMPANY.
AND NOW MOM'S IN THE HOSPITAL, AND NO ONE'S ALLOWED TO *SEE* HER?!
AND KAGAMI, HE SAID DAD DIED *PROTECTING* AYA!
MY SISTER SUDDENLY BECAME CERES AND ATTACKED ME, CALLING ME HER "MORTAL ENEMY."
AND SHE ACCUSED ME OF RAPE AND BEING A "CELESTIAL ROBE" THIEF!
TŌYA, YOU SAW... AND HEARD, DIDN'T YOU?

LOOK, I DON'T CARE WHAT YOU'RE SICK OF, OR IF IT BRINGS YOU TO TEARS OR WHAT...
...BUT LET ME SAY THIS...
WHAT THE HECK DID WE DO WRONG? DAMMIT...
THEY TOLD ME TO COOPERATE, TO HAVE NOTHING TO DO WITH AYA, OR THEY'D KILL HER! WHAT'S GOING ON?
AYA HAS BEEN SUFFERING THROUGH ALL OF THIS BY HERSELF.
AND YET SHE, TOO, TRIED TO PROTECT YOU FROM HARM.
LUCKILY, THE AOGIRIS TOOK HER IN.
WHILE YOU WERE BEING CODDLED BY THE MIKAGES, KEPT IGNORANT OF EVERY-THING...
...SHE WAS ALMOST KILLED BY THEM. AND YOUR DAD DIED FOR HER.

AND WHEN SHE TURNS INTO CERES— A DIFFERENT PERSON— IT'S *SHE* WHO SUFFERS THE MOST.
SHE'S STILL TRYING LIKE HELL TO FIGHT IT... TO DEFY HER FATE.
...AND YOU? YEAH, YOU DON'T LIKE IT, BUT WHAT'LL YOU *DO* ABOUT IT?
SIGH
I SURE RATTLE ON WHEN I'M WITH YOU GUYS.
AND IT WASN'T MY PLACE TO TALK, EITHER...
KNOCK KNOCK
TŌYA, YOU MUST REALLY CARE FOR...

EXCUSE ME, YOU TWO.
THE BOSS... KAGAMI WANTS YOU.
HEY, YOU'RE TŌYA, RIGHT?
I'M ALEXANDER O. HOWELL. I WORK UNDER KAGAMI!
CHECK IT: I'M INTO ANIME AND VIDEO GAMES. MY TYPE OF GIRL IS SHIORI IN "TOKIMEKI MEMORIAL!"
NICE TO MEET YOU.
..... I SEE.
BLINK
40 41 42 43 44 45 46 47 48 49 50
PLEASE WAIT HERE FOR A BIT.
...?

"THIS...IS MY SEAL... SO THAT YOU CAN STAY JUST THE WAY YOU ARE NOW."
I SUPPOSE IF WE GO ANY FURTHER, YOU'LL BE DISAPPOINTING THE BOYFRIEND WHO MADE THAT HICKEY.
!
HEY...
OR DID SOME MIDDLE-AGED PERV MAKE IT AS A PART OF A "PAID DATE" DEAL?
TŌYA!
SHUT UP!
DON'T PLAY GAMES WITH ME!
CERES IS STAYING BURIED! FOR... FOR AKI'S SAKE...

TŌ... YA!
I WON'T.
REALLY.
A--
IF YOU KEEP INSISTING ON HOLDING BACK... HOW ABOUT THIS?
HE WAS INSTRUCTED TO KEEP AN EYE ON YOU, BUT... I SEE.
TŌYA?

TAKE A LOOK AT YOUR NEMESIS... CERES.
AYA?!
A--

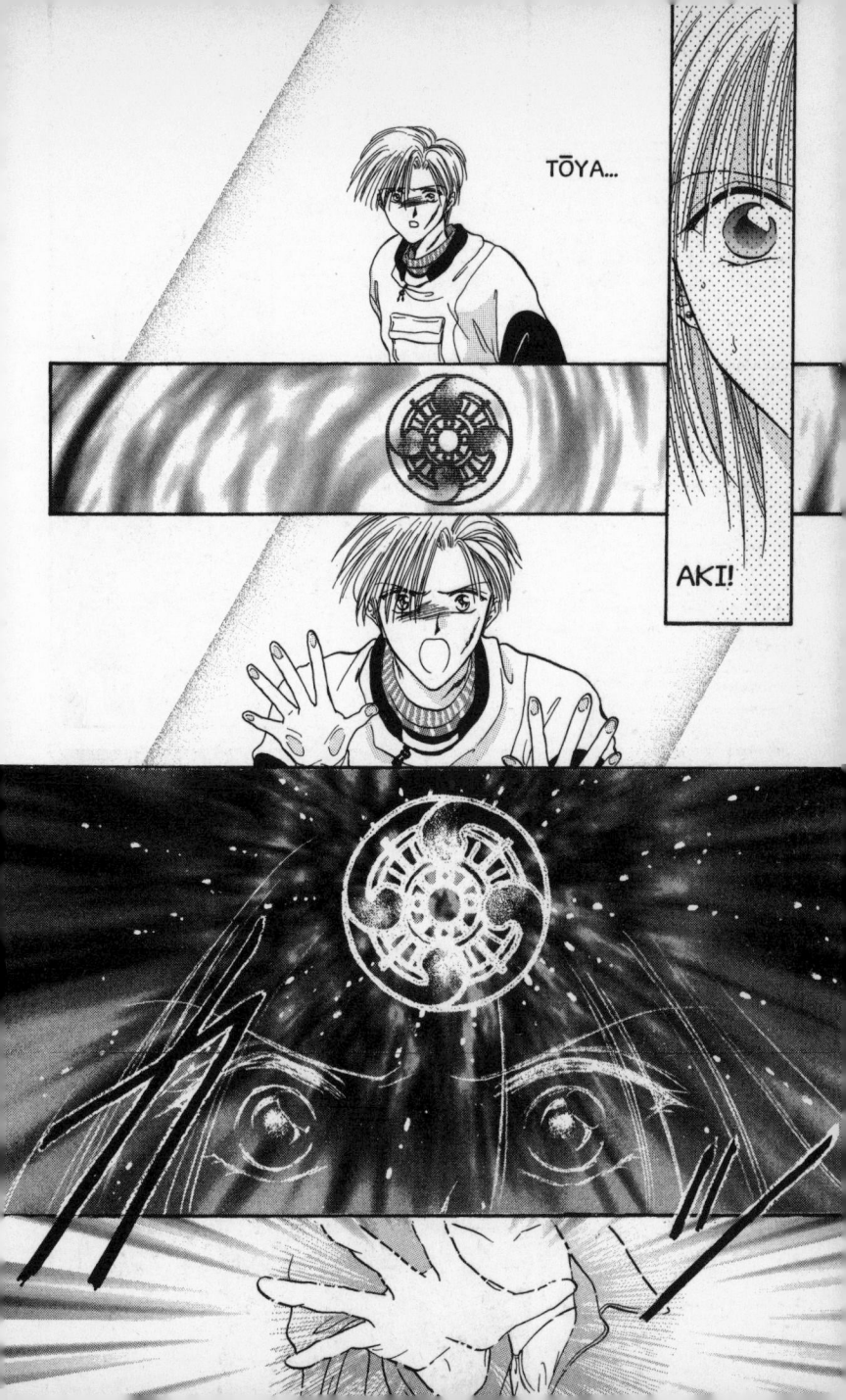
TŌYA...
AKI!

Ceres: 2

By the way, where I work, my assistants are whispering that Tōya is "a cyborg" or "an android." I guess that's a result of me trying not to make him very "human." ◡̈ I think a lot of people are thinking he's "aloof," but that's not quite right. It's just that he doesn't know how—or if he even has the capacity—to express his emotions. First of all, he doesn't know anything about himself, so it's not for other people to tell if he's kind, or cold... It's probably scary to not have any memories, and it would cause insecurity. So when Aya comes on to him so aggressively, does he really even know how to deal with it...? His memory will most likely serve as the crux of this story. (...Probably... um... ᘐ) My assistants are saying, "I bet he's like a totally irrelevant delivery guy or something!" (Of course not!) Tōya is a favorite of Assistant M., but she likes Kagami the best. She's on the Mikages' side. To her, "Yōhi's like, not even!"

She's not interested in younger men.

(But she was a fan of Tasuki in FY...) Assistant H. says, "Tōya and Yōhi are both good, but I feel sorry for Yōhi because it looks like he doesn't have a chance" (of ending up with Aya). K. is all into "Aki!" I don't know about S., but she says, "Yōhi is cute, kind of like an Akita." My editor says, "Alec is good," but I wonder what he thinks is good about him.

And why didn't he choose a girl?

Well, anyway... (I get distracted by X-Files on TV) ... (still distracted)... This genre is so interesting. What else--oh, Tokumei Research 200x ("Hot Topic Research 200X") is good too! And Takeshi no Banbutsu Soseiki ("Takeshi's Book of All Things Genesis")... I don't watch much typical family drama these days... But Odoru Daisosasen ("The Dancing Line of Criminal Investigation") is good too. Yeah. Oh!

I also watch Stalkers: Nigekirenu Ai ("Stalkers: Inescapable Love")!

...It's scary though...

The acting is so good.

!!!
THAT'S SPECIAL REINFORCED GLASS. THE SURROUNDING WALLS WEREN'T SO STURDY, THOUGH.
IT'S OK, YOU TWO.
!
SO, CERES, YOU'RE FINALLY OUT. HOW WAS THE TASTE OF THE GAS? YOU SHOULD NOW FEEL NUMB, AND UNABLE TO...
...MOVE
WHAT... ARE YOU GOING TO DO WITH ME, NOW THAT YOU'VE BROUGHT ME OUT? ARE YOU GOING TO HAVE YOUR *WAY* WITH ME, AS BEFORE?

...HE... MIKAGE TOOK MY CELESTIAL ROBES FROM ME. I WAS FORCED TO BE HIS WIFE... AND BORE HIS CHILDREN...
AND WE ARE THEIR DESCEND-ANTS.
I WILL CONTINUE TO REINCARNATE INTO THE ONES WITH MY BLOOD... THE GIRLS BORN INTO THE MIKAGES...INTO THE GIRLS WHO MOST SATISFY THE REQUIREMENTS FOR MY BODY... UNTIL I HAVE MY REVENGE!
!
...AS THAT MAN DID?
IS AKI... DOES HE EMBODY THE ONE WHO TOOK THE CELESTIAL ROBES FROM YOU?
...YES...
WHAT ABOUT YOU? WHY DO YOU EXIST IN AYA?

...I WAS THUS REBORN MANY TIMES. BUT UNTIL AGE 16 "I" COULD NOT FULLY AWAKEN AND I CANNOT HANDLE THE BODY WELL.
"WHO MOST SATISFIES THE REQUIREMENTS FOR YOUR BODY...?" BY APPEARANCE? OR...AH, YOU MEAN ONES WITH THE CLOSEST GENETIC MAKEUP.
THEN... I WILL AGAIN BE A COMPLETE CELESTIAL MAIDEN AND RETURN TO HEAVEN, UNHAMPERED BY AYA'S CONSCIOUS-NESS...
BUT NO MATTER... I WILL TAKE BACK MY CELESTIAL ROBES... BEFORE I DESTROY YOU ALL.
ドン!
YOU PEOPLE... FIGURED THAT OUT, AND RETURNED ME TO OBLIVION MANY TIMES, CALLING IT "RITUAL!" ...BUT THIS TIME, FINALLY...
...THAT AYA WILL DISAPPEAR?
...D-DOES THAT MEAN
YET... HOW IRONIC...THAT THAT DETESTABLE MAN WAS ALSO REBORN, AND IN MY TWIN... BORN AS MY SIBLING!

I KNOW NOTHING ABOUT YOUR CELESTIAL ROBES, AND I HAVE NOTHING TO DO WITH THE MIKAGES! YOU JUST LEAVE MY SISTER ALONE, YOU HEAR ME? GIVE HER BACK!
YOU'RE THE ONE WHO SHOULD DISAPPEAR!
EVEN IF THAT STORY IS TRUE, I'M ME! I DON'T HAVE ANY MEMORIES OF THAT GUY!
.....
WELL, IN ANY CASE, IT'S IMPOSSIBLE FOR YOU TO DESTROY THE FAMILY.
WHAT ARE YOU... DON'T TOUCH ME...
YOU SHOULD SLEEP A WHILE...

HOLD IT!
AOGIRI!
YŪ... HI...!
HANG ON TO ME!
BACK AWAY FROM AYA, SLOWLY...!
HOW DID YOU GET INSIDE...?

Yuhi
?!
WHA--

WAH HEH HEH
SHE...
SHE FLEW.
SHE SURE DID!

NOT GONNA TELL!
PORINKY PORINKY

.....

WHERE'S Q-CHAN?! WHERE'S THE GHOST?

YUP, SHE FLEW!
I MEAN, DID YOU SEE THAT?! ...SHE DEFINITELY...

...WHO ARE YOU?
.....

I'D FIRE YOU IF YOU WEREN'T A GENIUS WITH AN IQ OF 260!
I TOLD YOU NOT TO INPUT ANIME CHARACTER FACES IN THE SECURITY ACCESS DATABASE!
...ALEC... I GET IT NOW.
HE'S GONE ALREADY! MAYBE BECAUSE HE'S A GHOST?!
I CANNOT RETURN TO THE HEAVENS BY SIMPLE FLIGHT. AND I DON'T WANT TO STAY IN THIS UGLY PLACE...
I CAN UNDERSTAND HOW YOU FEEL! BUT AKI DOESN'T REMEMBER ANYTHING ABOUT THE CELESTIAL ROBES!
HEY! IF YOU CAN FLY, YOU DON'T NEED CELESTIAL ROBES!
THANK YOU FOR SAVING ME, YŪHI...
I HATE THIS!
LEMME DOWN! LEMME DOWN!
AND THINK ABOUT AYA'S LIFE FOR A SECOND! SHE KNOWS THERE ARE GOOD THINGS HERE, BECAUSE SHE BELONGS HERE! LIVE AS AYA AND LET BYGONES BE BYGONES!

SIGH.
SO YOU PREFER AYA THAT MUCH.
ALL RIGHT... I'LL GO BACK.
HUH...?

MOMMYYY!!
...KAGAMI!

NO! NOT HERE...
IDIOT!

HUH...?

I'LL COOPERATE WITH YOU... SO LONG AS THIS IS ABOUT GETTING AYA BACK TO NORMAL!
AKI?
I'VE DECIDED. I...WANT TO KNOW MORE ABOUT MYSELF...AND ABOUT THE CELESTIAL ROBES!
CERES ALWAYS SEEMS TO COME OUT WHEN SHE SEES ME. I'LL STAY AWAY FROM AYA UNTIL WE GET RID OF CERES.
ALL RIGHT...
"COOPERATE," HUH...!
I TRUST YOU GOT HER VISUALS ON THE BACKUP MONITOR?
AND HERE, ANALYZE THE BLOOD I GOT FROM HER.

THE CELESTIAL PROJECT...?
SHALL WE INITIATE THE "C-PROJECT"-- "C" FOR CELESTIAL, THAT IS?
SO, ARE YOU GOING TO DO WHAT AKI WANTS?
THE CELESTIAL MAIDEN WILL ONE DAY BE OURS.
I'LL BE LOOKING *FORWARD* TO IT... CERES...
AKI IS OUR TRUMP CARD WITH CERES. *OUR* PRIORITIES DON'T INVOLVE GETTING RID OF SUCH A FINE SPECIMEN OF A CELESTIAL MAIDEN. SO...
THAT'S IT! I'LL FIND *SOME* WAY TO MAKE AYA A NORMAL HUMAN BEING AGAIN, NO MATTER *WHAT* IT TAKES!
IT'S THAT, OR SOONER OR LATER *I'LL* END UP *DEAD!*
HUFF HUFF
WOW! GOOD THING YOU FELL INTO THE HOTEL POOL!

THESE ARE IMAGES OF AN *ACTUAL* CELESTIAL MAIDEN.
AS YOU CAN SEE, SHE EXHIBITS SUPERNATURAL ABILITIES...
...ACCOMPANIED BY CHANGES IN THE COLOR OF HER EYES AND HAIR.

HER CELESTIAL ASPECT IS "CERES."
HER HUMAN ASPECT IS 16-YEAR-OLD AYA MIKAGE...
セレス—CERES
御景 妖—AYA MIKA
NOW...I WOULD LIKE TO GO OVER WHAT YOU PERHAPS ALREADY KNOW.
YOU WOULDN'T THINK SO... SHE LOOKS LIKE YOUR TYPICAL TEENAGER.
CERES? THE ROMAN NAME FOR THE GODDESS DEMETER?
THE TALE OF THE CELESTIAL MAIDEN--THE "HAGOROMO LEGEND"--IS KNOWN AS "THE SWAN MAIDEN" IN EUROPE.
VARIATIONS OF THE STORY EXIST ALL OVER THE WORLD, WITH THE EXCEPTION OF THE AFRICAN CONTINENT AND POLYNESIA.
IT IS WIDELY KNOWN IN THE AMERICAN CONTINENTS, NORTH AND CENTRAL ASIA, OCEANIA...

日本
JAPAN
...IS ESPECIALLY CONCENTRATED IN EUROPE AND ASIAN COUNTRIES SUCH AS JAPAN, CHINA, KOREA, INDONESIA, AND MICRONESIA
THE EXIST-ENCE OF THE LEGEND...
JAPAN IN PARTICULAR HAS SEEN THE LEGEND PERPETUATED IN ALMOST 50 LOCATIONS.
AKITA
YAMAGATA
NIIGATA
NAGANO
TOYAMA
GIFU
KYOTO
SHIGA
TOTTORI
OKAYAMA
HIROSHIMA
HYOGO
SHIMANE
FUKUOKA
HOKKAIDO
AOMORI
IWATE
MIYAGI
FUKUSHIMA
TOCHIGI
IBARAKI
SAITAMA
CHIBA
TOKYO
SHIZUOKA
AICHI
WAKAYAMA
EHIME
KOUCHI
KAGAWA
TOKUSHIMA
OKINAWA
OITA
KUMAMOTO
...WHOSE BLOODLINES ARISE FROM WHAT THESE LEGENDS RELATE, ALL OVER JAPAN...AND EVEN THE WORLD.
IN OTHER WORDS, THERE IS A POSSIBILITY OF THE EXISTENCE OF OTHER CELESTIALS...
THE MIKAGE FAMILY IS THE ORIGIN OF ONE OF THEM...AND CERES HAS NOW SHOWN US THE TRUTH BEHIND THAT LEGEND.

MEANING, THE PEOPLE WHO HAD TAKEN THE CELESTIAL ROBES AND ACQUIRED THE CELESTIAL MAIDENS AND THEIR BLESSINGS IN VARIOUS PARTS OF THE WORLD BECAME HUMANITY'S CHOSEN HEROES... THEIR LEADERS.
THE HEAVENS GAVE THE ANCIENT PEOPLE WEALTH AND POWER THROUGH UNIONS WITH CELESTIAL MAIDENS.
THEY DEVELOPED A CULTURE AS "HUMAN BEINGS" THAT SURPASSED THOSE OF THE APES.
SO THIS TIME, THE MIKAGES ALONE WERE CHOSEN OUT OF ALL HUMANITY...
...FOR THIS HONOR.
御景 明
AKI MIKAGE
YES. THE MIKAGES NOW HAVE IN THEIR POSSESSION NOT ONLY A CELESTIAL MAIDEN, BUT THAT "CHOSEN LEADER."
MANKIND ONLY NEEDS ONE SUCH LEADER TODAY...

THAT'S RIGHT. AND TO START, WE'LL GATHER UP EVERYONE IN JAPAN WHO POSSESSES CELESTIAL GENES.
HOW WILL YOU IDENTIFY THESE PEOPLE?
WE'RE COLLECTING DATA AND COMPILING A LIST. ALL ON THAT LIST WILL BE CALLED "C-GENOMES."
WHAT ABOUT CERES... AYA MIKAGE?
UNFORTUNATELY, ALL WE HAVE AT THIS TIME IS A SAMPLE OF HER BLOOD.
SAITAMA
THE TIME HAS COME AGAIN TO RECEIVE THE ANGEL'S BLESSINGS...
AS THE MEN IN THE LEGENDS DID WHAT WAS NECESSARY...

"THE NEW CELESTIAL LEGEND..." THIS IS THE C-PROJECT, HUH...?
...EACH AND EVERY ONE OF YOU CHOSEN FOR THIS PROJECT WILL TAKE PART IN *CREATING* A LEGEND.
AND IT'S TO BE THE STORY OF HOW JUST ONE GUY ACQUIRES THE CELESTIAL MAIDENS OF THE ENTIRE COUNTRY? WHAT THE HECK ARE YOU GUYS *THINKING?*
YOU AND AYA LOVE EACH OTHER, DON'T YOU?
THAT'S NOT YOUR CONCERN.
INSTEAD, YOU SHOULD CAREFULLY CONSIDER YOUR *OWN* STATUS. YOU KNOW YOU'VE BEEN INCORPORATED INTO THIS PROJECT.
WHAT...?

IN ANY CASE, AYA AND AKI ARE COMFORTABLE WITH YOU. YOU CAN CONTINUE TO MONITOR HER.
.....
YOU DID DISCOVER WHAT IT'S LIKE TO *LOVE* SOMEONE, RIGHT?
HEH.
I'VE NEVER SEEN THAT EXPRESSION ON YOUR FACE BEFORE.
WHAT ARE YOU BABBLING ABOUT?
SEE? WE HAVE MORE THAN 100 KINDS!
HERE, TŌYA, PICK YOUR FAVORITE SET OF *MEMORIES!*
TA DA AA A!
KNOWLEDGE —INFORMATION— WILL BE TEMPORARILY INPUT INTO YOUR BRAIN... LITERALLY "MEMORY DATA."
ONE OF YOU'VE ENOUGH, ALEC.
YOU CAN EVEN BECOME A GAMER OR AN ANIME OTAKU!
BUT THEY WON'T BE *YOUR* MEMORIES.
WE WILL GIVE YOU THE ONES YOU'LL NEED TO BE ABLE TO STAY CLOSE TO AYA.
100 KINDS...
OF MEMORIES?

LISTEN, TŌYA... THIS PROJECT IS TOP SECRET...
...AND IF YOU BETRAY US, I'M AFRAID YOU WILL HAVE TO BE ELIMINATED... YOU UNDERSTAND?
"YOU DID DISCOVER WHAT IT'S LIKE TO LOVE SOMEONE, RIGHT?"
LOVE...?
MIKAGE...
...AYA...

SNXZZNNGGGHH
MIKAGE!
YOU MAY BE HAVING AFTER-LUNCH DOLDRUMS, BUT IN *MY* CLASS, YOU STAY AWAKE AND PAY ATTENTION!
AYA MIKAGE!
PLINK
OW!
SHNORR
MORON.
SWIP
OTHERWISE YOU *VOLUNTEER* TO CLEAN THE PHYSICS LAB AFTER SCHOOL! BY YOURSELF!
WE'RE IN THE GROOVE THESE DAYS...

ANYWAY, HOW CAN HE EXPECT ANYONE TO FULLY FOCUS DURING 5TH AND 6TH PERIODS!
...JUST BECAUSE I TOOK A LITTLE NAP!
WHAT WAS WITH THAT GUY? MR. SPECIAL LECTURER, ALL UPTIGHT...
YOU'RE IN THE WAY! GET WITH IT, WILLYA?
...JUST DON'T GET IN OUR WAY.
I'D GET MAD IF I WERE LECTURING AND A STUDENT CORKED OFF LIKE THAT!
GRUMP!
ALL BECAUSE THIS HEADBAND STOPS ME FROM GOING OFF ON MY OWN!
BUT PHYSICS IS JUST BORING!
HMPH!
BORING IS HAVING TO HELP YOU CLEAN UP THE PHYSICS LAB!

PHEW!
WE'RE FINALLY DONE! I'LL PUT THE CLEANING SUPPLIES AWAY, YOU GO RETURN THE KEY!
YES, SIR.
WHAT'S MADE HIM SO GRUMPY LATELY?
I MEAN, AT THE MOMENT I CAN'T BLAME HIM, BUT...
...TEACHER...
oh

PRODUCTION DIARY

...Anyway, all you elementary and middle high schoolers who don't know about genetics, don't worry! You'll learn about it in high school bio.
But there will be a lot of applications (?!) for genetics in the coming age, so I think it's good to know about it. Besides, it's more realistic than talking about "the blood of so-and-so."
It's incredible that all life is created from a blueprint that consists of just **four** nucleotides. This blueprint is called DNA (not the CD single by Makoto Kawamoto)... So even human beings take their shape according to the information encoded in DNA...
Oh! On another note, what's with the comment "Your self-portraits (on the "about the author" page in vol.1) have gotten cuter"...? That's **Aya!** ☺
Also, **Aya's picture** somehow ended up in the profile page in Yutopia Collections vol.1 "Delicious Studies" due to an editing error! I'm not so stupid that I would beautify my self-portrait that much! ☺ It was a mistake! Besides, I have short hair now. Sheesh! ✧
Well, not much room left. See you in the next volume. Oh, about "the title illustrations being left out"--that's because Ceres doesn't have chapter titles. So there won't be any. I'll try to clump them in the extra pages at the end of the graphic novels.

Bye.

I just heard from my editor that Datahouse is coming out with a book called "Fushigi Yûgi's Mysterious Secrets"!

WHO ARE YOU TALKING ABOUT?
NOBODY. FORGET IT.
WHAT'S WITH YŪHI?
HE'S STILL SUSPICIOUS OF TŌYA AFTER AN ENTIRE MONTH? AND WHY SHOULD THAT PUT HIM IN A BAD MOOD?
AYA, GO TO SLEEP!
I KNOW!
HE DOESN'T KNOW WHAT I'M GOING THROUGH... I RESEARCH THE LEGENDS EVERY NIGHT, BUT THERE'S NOTHING THAT TELLS ME HOW I CAN RETURN TO NORMAL...
AND KEEPING CERES FROM COMING OUT AT SCHOOL IS WEARING ME OUT.
STILL, IF NOTHING MORE HAPPENS, MAYBE MY LIFE CAN BE NORMAL ENOUGH...

"MAY IT HELP YOU *WIN* THE FIGHT FOR YOURSELF. THEN..."
ARE YOU STAYING BY AKI'S SIDE? DO YOU REMEMBER *ME* SOME-TIMES...?
THERE'S A TON OF THINGS I HAVE TO THINK ABOUT... BUT HE KEEPS POPPING INTO MY HEAD.
THE MARK...IT FADED LONG AGO, TŌYA.
IT MUST MEAN THAT I LOVE HIM AFTER ALL... OH, BROTHER.
NEXT TIME, JUST *SAY* WHAT YOU HAVE TO SAY... TŌYA...

YEAH, RIGHT! AFTER *YOU* THREATEN TO KILL ME SO *DEAD* IF I STEP INTO YOUR ROOM IN THE MIDDLE OF THE NIGHT?
YOU COULD'VE TURNED IT OFF!
AS IF I COULD SLEEP WITH YOUR LIGHT ON ALL NIGHT!
YOU TOO, YŪHI? HOW COULD *YOU* OVER-SLEEP!
I OVER-SLEPT!
I WOULDN'T PEEP AT *YOU* IF YOU *PAID* ME!
YOU KNOW, I TRY TO WATCH MY BACK WHEN I TAKE A BATH, CHANGE CLOTHES, AND GO TO BED.
SO YOU'RE SO HIGH STRUNG YOU CAN'T SLEEP BECAUSE OF A STUPID LIGHT?
HEH HEH HEH
IT ISN'T THE LIGHT IN THE ROOM THAT'S BOTHERING YOU, YŪHI, IT'S THE OCCUPANT!
PUBERTY, YOU KNOW. CHUCKLE...

WHAT'S UP?
.....
HMMM... JUST THINKING HOW THE GIRLS ALL HAVE BLEACHED HAIR AND LOOSE SOCKS.
HMPH! SO DO YOU!
BUT WHEN I LOOK AT IT FROM HERE, I REALIZE THAT OUT THERE I'D BE LIKE THEM, JUST ANOTHER CLONE.
BUT, AND I KNOW I SOUND CONTRADICTORY, I'D FEEL COMFORTABLE... JUST BECAUSE I WAS LIKE EVERYONE ELSE.
YEAH... BUT I ALWAYS KINDA THOUGHT THOSE THINGS HELPED ME EXPRESS MY INDIVIDUALITY!
I GUESS THAT COMES FROM BEING DIFFERENT NOW. I MIGHT LOOK THE SAME, BUT THERE AREN'T ANY TEENAGERS LIKE...
HA HA HA
LIKE I WAS LOST WITHIN THE PACK...

WHAT...?
A GIRL...
YES?!
MRS. Q, TURN RIGHT!
SHE'S BURNING...

OH...
WH-WHAT'S WRONG?
STOP RIGHT *THERE!*
HEY! ARE YOU ALL RIGHT?!
AYA, SHE *FELL!* DON'T MOVE HER!
WHAT SHOULD WE DO? GET HER TO THE HOSPITAL...?
I...IT'S YŪKI, FROM CLASS 3!

TO SCHOOL...
TAKE ME TO SCHOOL. I JUST FELT A LITTLE WOOZY... AND TRIPPED...
YŪKI?!
NURSE'S OFFICE
I HOPE SHE'S OKAY...
WHAT NOW? CLASS IS STARTING.
YOU GO AHEAD, TELL THE TEACHER WHAT HAPPENED. I'M GOING TO STAY WITH HER.

HOW DID YOU KNOW SHE WAS THERE, ANYWAY?
I... GOT A VISION...
IT WAS WEIRD. JUST FOR A MOMENT, IT LOOKED LIKE SHE WAS ENVELOPED IN *FLAMES*...
GOD!
EVER SINCE THIS CELESTIAL MAIDEN BUSINESS STARTED, I'VE DISCOVERED ALL THESE POWERS. GUESS IT INCLUDES SOME TYPE OF ESP.
SO MUCH FOR HOPING NOTHING MORE WOULD HAPPEN, THAT I COULD BE NORMAL. I'M SUCH A *WEIRDO!*
WELL, LIKE YOU SAID, THERE CERTAINLY AREN'T ANY TEENAGERS LIKE *YOU!*
OUCH
GREAT! *NOW* YOU AGREE WITH ME!

THERE ISN'T ANYONE WITH *GUTS* LIKE YOU, EITHER!
ANYWAY...
SO YOU HAVE A FEW NEW TALENTS. NOTHING WRONG WITH THAT.
NOT MANY PEOPLE WALK BY THAT ALLEY, SO IF YOU HADN'T ENVISIONED YŪKI, AND SHE'D HIT HER HEAD, SHE'D HAVE BEEN IN *SERIOUS* TROUBLE.

"IT ISN'T THE LIGHT... BOTHERING YOU... IT'S THE OCCUPANT!"
Mrs.
YOU'RE NOT A WEIRDO, OKAY? SO CHEER UP.
HE KNEW...?
NOT TO MENTION FALLING ASLEEP IN CLASS MORE OFTEN.
SO TAKE IT EASY! YOU'LL WEAR YOURSELF OUT WORRYING AND STARING AT BOOKS ABOUT CELESTIAL MAIDENS EVERY NIGHT.
!
N-NO WAY...
HE WOULDN'T...
AYA...
...BE FEELING SUCH...
...SAY...
CLASS...

...IS STARTING, YOU GUYS.
WAAAAH!
QUIET! WHAT'S GOING ON IN HERE?
DON'T SHOUT IN THE INFIRMARY, YOU IDIOT.
WHY! WHY ARE YOU HERE?!
ANOTHER ILLUSION?!
WH...WHA!
TŌYA?!

SCHOOL DOCTOR...
NICE TO MEET YOU.
OUR NEW SCHOOL PHYSICIAN. HE'S TAKING OVER FOR DR. YOSHIHARA, WHO WAS TRANSFERRED ELSEWHERE.
DR. MIKAMI.
NURSE, HE'S...
COME WITH ME!
NO WAY!
DON'T LET HIM FOOL YOU! HE'S A MINION OF EVIL OUT TO CAPTURE THE CELESTIAL MAIDEN!
HUH?
KAGAMI SET ME UP WITH A FICTITIOUS IDENTITY, COMPLETE WITH BIRTH RECORDS AND PERSONAL HISTORY.
B-B-BUT STILL... HOW?!
THIS IS A NICE SCHOOL, AYA. THEIR MEDICAL FACILITIES ARE FIRST RATE.

EVEN BETTER, THEY'VE IMPLANTED EXTENSIVE MEDICAL KNOWLEDGE INTO MY BRAIN. THERE WEREN'T ANY MEMORIES TAKING UP SPACE IN THERE ANYWAY...
...SO I'M A BLANK, ABLE TO ASSUME ANY GUISE.
Y...YOU CAN *DO* THAT...?
KAGAMI... HE'S SCARY.
IS...
...IS THAT... SO YOU COULD... STAY CLOSE TO ME?
HE CAN CREATE PEOPLE AS HE LIKES...AND ELIMINATE THEM TOO...

I DON'T CARE IF YOU WERE ORDERED TO.
I WANTED TO SEE YOU...
I'M SO WARM...
ALL MY FATIGUE IS MELTING AWAY. IT'S STRANGE...
...AS IF MY BODY IS FILLED WITH NEW STRENGTH...
...IT'S COMING FROM *INSIDE* ME...

I SAID, HE'S NOT A DOCTOR! HE'S NOT ANYTHING!
I'M FINE!
AOGIRI, WAS IT? YOU SHOULD GET SOME REST! I'LL GET DR. MIKAMI TO LOOK AT YOUR HEAD. OK?
DON'T YELL! YOU'LL WAKE MY OTHER PATIENT.
AYA...
...HERE'S MY REPLY... FROM LAST TIME.

WHAT...?
!?
AYA, MY SOLE CONCERN IS CERES.
DON'T EXPECT ANYTHING FROM ME ANYMORE.
TO BE CONTINUED IN VOLUME 3: SUZUMI

The Ceres Guide to Sound Effects

We've left most of the sound effects in CERES as Yuu Watase originally created them – in Japanese.

VIZ has created this glossary to help you decipher, page-by-page and panel-by-panel, what all those foreign words and background noises mean. Use this guide to impress your friends with your new Japanese vocabulary.

The glossary lists the page number then panel. For example, 3.1 indicates page 3, panel 1.

15.1 FX: Za (shake)
15.2 FX: Suu (float)

18.1 FX: Ha (wah)
18.2 FX: Sa (color retreating)

19.5 FX: Uuu fan fan fan (sound of sirens)

20.1 FX: Pii poo fan fan (sound of sirens)
20.2 FX: Ta (dash)

21.7 FX: Kacha (click)

26.2 FX: Gashi (grab)

27.3 FX: Don (slam)

33.4 FX: Dosa (thud)

34.1 FX: Peta (step)
34.4 FX: Yoro yoro (wobble wobble)

35.3 FX: Kotsu kotsu kotsu (thup thup thup)

37.3 FX: Katsu katsu (thup thup)

39.3 FX: Karari (rattle)

40.5 FX: Zuki (throb)

6.4 FX: Pero (lick)
6.5 FX: Niko (grin)

7.1 FX: Jiri (step)
7.3 FX: Ba (crash)
7.5 FX: Garan (clatter)

8.1 FX: Za (shake)

9.3 FX: Don (boom)

10.1 FX: Garan (crumble)
10.1 FX: Suto (thump)
10.3 FX: Fu (fading)
10.4 FX: Fuwa (float)
10.6 FX: Gyo (urk)

11.1 FX: Biku (uh)
11.2 FX: Fuwa (float)

12.1 FX: Suu (descending)
12.4 FX: Ta (tump)
12.6 FX: Poon (bounce)

13.1 FX: Poon (bounce)
13.2 FX: Poon (bounce)
13.2 FX: Poon (bounce)
13.3 FX: Koro koro koro (roll roll roll)
13.4 FX: Pita (stopping)
13.5 FX: Ba (fwash)

14.1 FX: Giriri (squirm)

63.2 FX: Kasa kasa (rustle rustle)
63.3 FX: Gashi (grab)

64.1 FX: Kasa (rustle)
64.2 FX: Kasa (rustle)

68.2 FX: Gyu (clench)

69.5 FX: Suu (zzzzz)
69.6 FX: Gyu (squeeze)

70.3 FX: Fu (shwwuuh)

71.1 FX: Gu (choke)

72.1 FX: Basa (fwump)
72.4 FX: Giri giri (squeeze squeeze)

73.3 FX: Ba (spring)

74.2 FX: Jiji (jolt)
74.4 FX: Geho geho geho (cough cough cough)
74.5 FX: Dota dota dota (tump tump tump)

75.1 FX: Gara (rattle)

76.3 FX: Ba (crash)

77.4 FX: Da (swoosh)

78.4 FX: Don (shove)

79.1 FX: Zuki (throb)
79.6 FX: Gara (rattle)

81.2 FX: Ga (grab)

83.5 FX: Biki (crunch)

85.2 FX: Buroro (vroom)

86.3 FX: Ba (slip)

41.3 FX: Zuka zuka zuka (stomp stomp stomp)
41.4 FX: Gara (rattle)

42.1 FX: Dota dota dota dota (tromp tromp tromp tromp)

44.2 FX: Kaa kaa (sound of crows)

45.2 FX: Pita (click)
45.4 FX: Kasa (rustle)

47.1 FX: Goron (roll)

48.3 FX: Kara (rattle)
48.4 FX: Suu (zzzzz)

49.1 FX: Zoku (wooo)

51.1 FX: Yoro (stagger)
51.2 FX: Don (thump)
51.4 FX: Don (bump)

52.2 FX: Zuki (throb)
52.4 FX: Ga (yank)

53.1 FX: Gaku (slump)
53.2 FX: Doka ga (kick)
53.2 FX: Ga (whack)
53.5 FX: Ga (grab)

54.1 FX: Zuzaa (fling)
54.3 FX: Dogu (whack)

55.2 FX: Koso koso koso (shuffle shuffle shuffle)

56.3 FX: Yoro yoro (wobble wobble)
56.4 FX: Ga (yank)

59.2 FX: Gacha (kerchak)

60.5 FX: Patan (slam)

123.1 FX: Pa (blink)
123.4 FX: Vii (elevator whir)
123.5 FX: Pa (blink)
123.6 FX: Goon (stop)

124.3 FX: Gakon (clunk)

125.1 FX: Sha (swipe)

127.1 FX: Don (shove)
127.2 FX: Bamu (slam)
127.3 FX: Bi (snag)

129.2 FX: Gacha gacha (rattle rattle)
129.5 FX: Hyoi hyoi (ta-tap ta-tap)

130.1 FX: Jii (whir)
130.3 FX: Gaa (rattle)

131.3 FX: Bi (rip)
131.2 FX: Pan (slap)
131.3 FX: Ta (dash)
131.4 FX: Gachi (clack)
131.5 FX: Ngigi (grrrr)

133.3 FX: Doka (thunk)

134.1 FX: Dan (slam)
134.5 FX: Dokun (ba-bump)

135.1 FX: Buru buru buru (tremble tremble tremble)
135.3 FX: Giri (teeth grinding)
135.5 FX: Zaa (emanating power)

139.3 FX: Dosu (thump)

140.1 FX: Kacha (click)
140.6 FX: Pa (light blinking)

142.1 FX: Giri (scratch)
142.4 FX: Ha ha ha (huff huff huff)
142.5 FX: Su (vwip)
142.6 FX: Gakon (klunk)

90.5 FX: Patan (click)
90.6 FX: Pasa (flump)

91.1 FX: Gyu (clench)
91.2 FX: Kacha (click)
91.5 FX: Buru (brrr)

94.1 FX: Gishi (creak)
94.4 FX: Kata kata (tremble tremble)

96.1 FX: Kaa (blush)

97.2 FX: Gyu (squeeze)

106.2 FX: Yoro (stagger)

107.2 FX: Su (snatch)
107.5 FX: Sa (holding away)

108.2 FX: Dota dota dota dota dota dota dota (vroom vroom vroom vroom vroom vroom vroom)
108.3 FX: Kukaa (zzzz)
108.4 FX: Guwara (zhoop)

109.1 FX: Boki boki (knuckles cracking)

113.3 FX: Rrrrr (ring)

115.4 FX: Pushu (elevator whir)
115.5 FX: Pa (tug)

116.1 FX: Daa (dash)

118.4 FX: Gaa (rattle)
118.5 FX: Kacha (click)
118.5 FX: Rrrrr (ring)

119.1 FX: Kacha (click)

120.3 FX: Ton ton (tap tap)

122.2 FX: Gashaan (slam)

165.2 FX: Kacha (click)
165.3 FX: Suu (zzzzzz)

166.5 FX: Zuri (slurp)

169.2 FX: Jii (squint)

170.3 FX: Don (bam)

171.4 FX: Suu (zzzzz)
171.5 FX: Chichi (chirp)

172.1 FX: Dotatata (vroooom)

174.1 FX: Biku (aah)
174.3 FX: Ba (foomph)
174.4 FX: Gyururu (screech)

175.2 FX: Kikii (screech)
175.4 FX: Za (fwump)
175.5 FX: Piku (twitch)

176.1 FX: Ga (grab)

178.1 FX: Doki (ba-bump)

179.4 FX: Dokun dokun
(ba-bump ba-bump)

180.2 FX: Kiin (aiyee)

181.4 FX: Gashi (tug)

183.1 FX: Kyu (squeeze)

184.2 FX: Doki (ba-bump)
184.5 FX: Suu (zzzzz)
184.6 FX: Chiri chiri (crackle crackle)

185.2 FX: Bou (foomph)

143.1 FX: Suu (whir)
143.2 FX: Gakon (klunk)

144.5 FX: Ka (flash)

145.1 FX: Zuun (boom)
145.2 FX: Shu (spray)

146.2 FX: Byooo (whoosh)

148.3 FX: Zuru (stagger)
148.5 FX: Byoo (whoosh)

149.4 FX: Su (tapping syringe)
149.6 FX: Shu (burst)

150.1 FX: Ton (poke)
150.4 FX: Yoro (stagger)

151.1 FX: Su (reach)
151.2 FX: Zawa (murmur)
151.4 FX: Ba (leap)

152.2 FX: Byoo (whoosh)

153.6 FX: Ba (shoom)

154.1 FX: Byoo (whoosh)
154.3 FX: Hishi (clutch)

156.5 FX: Patan (click)

158.3 FX: Zawa zawa (murmur murmur)

159.1 FX: Pa (blip)

160.1 FX: Katan (rising)
160.4 FX: Kotsu kotsu (footsteps)

161.4 FX: Pa (blip)

164.2 FX: Ta ta (scamper scamper)
164.2 FX: Kacha kacha (clink clink)

Yuu Watase was born on March 5 in a town near Osaka, Japan, and she was raised there before moving to Tokyo to follow her dream of creating manga. In the decade since her debut short story, *PAJAMA DE OJAMA* (An Intrusion in Pajamas), she has produced more than 50 compiled volumes of short stories and continuing series. Her latest work, *Zettai Kareshi* (Absolute Boyfriend), recently completed its run in Japan in the anthology magazine *Shôjo Comic*. Watase's other beloved series *Ceres: Celestial Legend, Fushigi Yûgi, Imadoki! (Nowadays),* and *Alice 19*™ are now available in North America in English editions published by VIZ.

Hell Hath No Fury Like a Heavenly Maiden

When an angel named Ceres is reincarnated in 16-year-old Aya Mikage, Aya becomes a liability to her family's survival. Not only does Ceres want revenge against the Mikage family for past wrongs, but her power is also about to manifest itself. Can Aya control Ceres' hold on her, or will her family mark her for death?

From Yuu Watase, creator of ALICE 19TH, FUSHIGI YÛGI, and IMADOKI!– complete your collection today!

CERES
Celestial Legend

Complete anime series on two DVD box sets– 12 episodes per volume

only $49.98 each!

viz media

www.viz.com
store.viz.com

©Yuu Watase / Shogakukan • Bandai Visual • Studio Pierrot

All 18 volumes of the popular manga series now available!

Also available: *Fushigi Yûgi: Genbu Kaiden*, from our Shojo Beat Manga line

Manga $9.99

Over 100 pieces of art, with drawings and paintings produced especially for this new edition, formatted to match the original Japanese book!

Art of $19.99

fushigi yûgi™

GET THE COMPLETE
FUSHIGI YÛGI COLLECTION
viz media
www.viz.com
store.viz.com
© 1992 Yuu WATASE/Shogakukan Inc.
© 1995 Yuu WATASE/Shogakukan Inc.

COVELY BRANCH

Collection

Complete your Angel Sanctuary collection—
buy the manga and art book today at store.viz.com!

Read the epic saga of forbidden love from the start—the 20-volume manga series now available.

A hardcover collection of illustrations from manga volumes 1-8, plus character info and an exclusive interview with creator Kaori Yuki.

www.viz.com
store.viz.com

Tenshi Kinryou Ku © Kaori Yuki 1994/HAKUSENSHA, Inc.
Yuki Kaori Gashu Tenshi Kinryou Ku Angel Cage by Kaori Yuki © Kaori Yuki 1997/HAKUSENSHA, Inc.

A Heavenly
Angel Sanctuary™

J
JAN 10
DETROIT PUBLIC LIBRARY
W9-CHY-148

The Sh

Let us know what you think!

CONELY BRANCH LIBRARY
4600 MARTIN
DETROIT, MI 48210
(313) 224-6461

MAR '10
RELEASE DETROIT PUBLIC LIBRARY

Help us make the manga you love better!

viz media

JAN © 2010

A-YORI DANGO © 1992 by Yoko Kamio/SHUEISHA Inc. Hanazakari no Kimitachi ha © Hisaya Nakajo 1996/HAKUSENSHA, Inc. RED RIVER © 1995 Chie SHINOHARA/Shogakukan Inc.